Bocconi University Press

Paolo Verri

THE URBAN PARADOX

Nine Cities in Search of the Future

Foreword by **Carlo Ratti**

Cover: Cristina Bernasconi, Milan
Typesetting: Laura Panigara, Cesano Boscone (MI)

EGEA S.p.A.
Via Salasco, 5 - 20136 Milano
Tel. 02/5836.5751 – Fax 02/5836.5753
egea.edizioni@unibocconi.it – www.egeaeditore.it

First edition: December 2025

ISBN Domestic Edition	979-12-80623-10-2
ISBN Digital Domestic Edition	979-12-229-8140-6
ISBN International Edition	978-88-31322-83-6
ISBN Digital International Edition	978-88-31322-84-3

To my family,
To my friends,
And to our journeys through cities.

Contents

Foreword, by *Carlo Ratti* IX

Introduction. The future belongs to the cities 1

1 Barcelona. From dictatorship to autonomy 25

2 Turin. From manufacturing to culture 41

3 Pittsburgh. Steel and disease 67

4 Lyon. The government of light 81

5 Milan. From politics to policies (and back) 97

6 Istanbul. Crossroads or monad? 117

7 Wrocław. A city for young people 133

8 Matera. From shame to pride 147

9 Tokyo. Old people and children 167

Conclusions. Putting cities back in the hands of the citizens 181

Bibliography 189

Foreword

by *Carlo Ratti**

Since the post-war period, few places in Italy have managed to transform their reputation in the eyes of international observers as radically as Matera and its surrounding region. For decades, a stigma hung over the area so deeply it seemed irreparable—beginning with the most famous of all literary references, Carlo Levi's *Christ Stopped at Eboli*. Yet in recent years, readers of major international newspapers have encountered a very different narrative. Just before the pandemic, *The Observer* described Matera as a "diamond in the rough," *Le Monde* spoke of a "revanche de Matera," and *The Times* crowned it the new "rock star of Italy," playing on the double meaning of "rock" in reference to the city's ancient *Sassi* dwellings.

Behind this chorus of enthusiasm lies the extraordinary work of an entire community, which in 2019 staged one of the most successful editions of the European Capital of Culture in the program's history—a collective achievement born of collaboration between politics, business, and civil society. Much of the credit, however, belongs to Paolo Verri, the driving force behind the entire enterprise.

Those who know Verri, as I do, are aware that his career had already reached remarkable milestones well before Matera 2019. In 2015, he directed the program of events for the Italian Pavilion at the Milan Expo. Many of the initiatives he has led have had Turin as their stage—from

* Architect and engineer, he heads the architecture firm CRA-Carlo Ratti Associati (Turin and New York) and founded the Senseable City Lab at MIT in Boston.

the Book Fair and the city's strategic plan to the promotion of the 2006 Winter Olympics—helping to give substance to that often-evoked yet elusive ideal of the "creative city." The publication of *The Urban Paradox* thus arrives at a timely moment, as Turin, after years of uncertainty, seeks once again to look to the future with confidence.

But what, exactly, is the paradox Verri describes—one that clearly transcends the borders of Piedmont? "A city," he writes, "is a tortoise of extraordinary longevity and beauty, to which no citizen will ever be an Achilles." The lesson, valid for administrators and planners alike, is that success and decline in an urban setting are inseparable: each generates and sustains the other. "A city," he warns, "can never say, 'I made it.'" In other words, "the myth of perfection—of a balanced society, of a fully responsible relationship between power and democracy, between wealth and redistribution—is in crisis." There is no perfect city, and no infallible citizen; only a dynamic, continuous relationship between the two. And this relationship embodies a paradox, mirroring Achilles' eternal pursuit of the tortoise.

Drawing on his Italian experience, Verri broadens his gaze to a series of international metropolises—Barcelona, Pittsburgh, Lyon, Istanbul, Wrocław, and Tokyo—that together outline the shared challenges of building the future. In the face of climate change, deindustrialization, automation, and geopolitical strain, the tools of culture may seem fragile. Yet they remain the essential ground on which identity, belonging, and, above all, civic participation can be rebuilt.

Accepting the paradox of cities does not mean rejecting change. As the author rightly observes, a "smart city" can hardly exist where "smart citizens" are lacking. Still, it would be mistaken to see digital innovation as serving only efficiency. The most interesting examples in this book show precisely how technology can be harnessed for inclusion and participation.

The chapters on Milan and Turin are particularly revealing when read together. A cosmopolitan *torinese*, Verri avoids the bitterness that has often marked local discourse. He regards the Lombard capital without envy, with curiosity—acknowledging both its strengths and its limits. With the end of the industrial era, both cities were forced to move beyond what had long defined their influence. Each pursued renewal through a major event—the 2006 Winter Olympics in Turin and Expo

2015 in Milan. But while Milan seized the opportunity to design a medium- and long-term revitalization plan, Turin settled for a temporary repositioning that quickly lost momentum. "Behold, Turin," Verri writes, "which loses Fiat and then returns to the top, loses everything again because its ruling class no longer has any external enemies, fights against itself and, like Cronos, eats its own children." The Savoy capital must again ignite a process of innovation—one that, in my view, should begin with a renewed alliance between Milan and Turin. From historical rivals to partners, they could form a single metropolitan axis spanning the entire northwest of Italy.

Ultimately, Verri's invitation is to use the leverage of "big events" as catalysts for lasting urban innovation—but only if they serve as the beginning of a broader, long-term transformation. Matera was able to reinvent itself as a European Capital of Culture precisely because it forged a new shared identity: from a cause of scandal to a source of pride. And even if the urban paradox remains—if Achilles still struggles to catch the tortoise—the two will at least have advanced together, covering a good part of the road.

Introduction
The future belongs to the cities

At the very beginning of his *Histories*, Herodotus comments on the past, present, and future of cities: "I shall go forward further with the story, giving an account of the cities of men, small as well as great: for those which in old times were great have for the most part become small, while those that were in my own time great used in former times to be small," he writes.

Twenty-three centuries of history indicate that there will always be work for those engaged in cities. This is partly because never in the history of mankind have cities been so numerous or so important. Until the year 2000, most of the planet's population lived in rural areas; it is only the 21st century that can truly be defined as urban. The predicted growth of cities over the coming years is astonishing. In 2030, 9 percent of the world's population will live in the world's thirty-three largest cities and 15 percent of the world's gross domestic product (GDP) will be produced in them. The largest "megacity" will be neither New York nor Moscow; it will be in neither Europe nor America, but in Asia. It will not be a Chinese city, as many might think; rather, the most populous city in the world will be Jakarta, the capital of Indonesia. By 2030, it will have no fewer than 35 million inhabitants, outnumbering Tokyo—which will have lost about 2 million residents by that time.

Twenty-six of the thirty-three largest cities in the world will be in developing countries: In Asia there will be nineteen, of which six will be in China and four in India. Some of today's best-known cities will continue to dominate the world scene: Cairo, for example, will have 30 million inhabitants, and Lagos will represent the rise of Africa in the first half of this century. African cities will be the world's youngest and most dynamic, with the highest economic growth. Osaka, in contrast, will be the most elderly city: Perhaps as much as 31 percent of its population will be aged over sixty-five.

"I've been around a lot of construction sites, in Italy and abroad. Sometimes you're buried under rules and regulations and treated as if you're a moron. At other times they let you do what the hell you want, because if you break your head, the insurance will pay for a new one." It is Libertino Faussone, the narrator of Primo Levi's book *The Wrench*, who speaks here. He builds cities piece by piece, from bridges to roads, and deals with real, concrete people, in a text that is almost the opposite of the pure mythology portrayed in Italo Calvino's *Invisible Cities.* Those who work in the city do not have time to theorize; they are obsessed with the relentless ticking of the clock. Yet they know that haste is waste; that the impact of many choices they make, of many jobs they undertake, will last for centuries, so mistakes are serious. And yet there is an almost incomprehensible frenzy among city workers, as if they are always trying to make up for lost time.

In Europe, since the 1990s, an almost physical urge to make cities fit for the future has permeated nation after nation: Great Britain and Spain, parts of Germany and Italy, even Eastern European countries, have been overwhelmed by the desire to transform their cities. This has been much more than pure restoration, imposed from above; it has also included bottom-up measures to prevent further destruction. These actions have revitalized and redeveloped dozens of urban spaces, even reintroducing rivers, parks, and gardens that industrial civilization had almost completely swept away.

For example, the heart of Turin's late 19th-century military district, between Europe's largest open-air market, Porta Palazzo, and the flea market that is held under the balconies of the Cottolengo Hospital, has been transformed into what can only be described as a green forest—just a few hundred meters from the Town Hall. The words of archaeologist C.W. Ceram come to mind: "Finding old masonry built by some long-vanished people somewhere in a strange forest is interesting enough and evokes all sorts of questions, but it is hardly right, one might say, to call it a miracle."[1] Yet for us Turinese who were then in our early thirties,

---

[1] C.W. Ceram, *Gods, Graves, and Scholars: The Story of Archaeology* (New York: Vintage Books, 1986, first published 1949).

the transformation of a symbol of war into an emblem of peace and development was just one element of a revolutionary makeover that brought back to life a city that had been diminished by forty years of industrialization. In early November 2019, this place was experienced by thousands of young people as an urban stage for one of Europe's most important festivals, Club To Club. It had become not only a musical space, but also a space for meeting, for commerce, for physical contact—a generator of passions and emotions.

Charles Landry, one of the most respected experts on urban development, has noted that "The city is an assault on the senses. Cities are sensory, emotional experiences, for good and for bad."[2] Successful urban development has to bear this in mind: Experiences, emotions, and sensations work together to create a distinctive urban feeling.

I have had the good fortune to be called upon by three administrations to try to reproduce successes that have been achieved in cities that differ in history, size, and their desire to compete and cooperate. It is almost as if they are football teams that buy a few champion players: Even if they do not win the championship, the presidents who hired them look good. But this is not the case with mayors, who recognize that their dialogue with citizens must be sincere and reciprocal. They must be authoritative in both giving and asking; both extraordinarily welcoming but also gently demanding of long-term residents and temporary citizens alike.

Redevelopment is not a minor challenge. It touches in concrete terms on the cultural landscape, on visitors' perceptions, on what we might refer to as "beauty maintenance." Just as one falls in love with a woman because of her natural beauty, perhaps enhanced by a subtle pair of earrings, not because of her use of cosmetics, so one instinctively loves a city because of its "bone structure" and the sensitive care of its greenery, streets, and buildings—not because it is an unhealthy copy of a theme park, its urban context turned into a "product."

Joseph Rykwert has written:

> A city whose dominant buildings are housing—and I mean housing for offices as well as apartments for people—will inevitably be short on public spaces and on monuments, whether the city develops horizontally or verti-

---

[2] Charles Landry, *The Art of City-Making* (London and Sterling: Earthscan, 2006).

> cally. Monuments will be dwarfed by their surroundings. Such a city will therefore also be short on places that might serve its inhabitants as landmarks, orientation guides, and "points of interest," or any other striking, easily identifiable features to use as meeting points.[3]

Over the coming years, cash injections made in the 2014–2020 period will have to be integrated with the European Commission's economic plans for the period 2021–2027 and the proper use of funds from Italy's National Recovery and Resilience Plan to deal with the aftermath of the COVID-19 pandemic. It feels as if Europe has consciously identified two phases in the development of cities: containers and content, or perhaps bricks and mortar and an underlying nervous system. The two have to go hand in hand in terms of planning and reporting: A master plan has to be developed alongside strategic development. Failing to do this is like looking at the human body in terms of the skeleton and then in relation to musculature—but not both at the same time.

Today, thanks to integrated information systems, we can involve all citizens during all their daily activities. We can work with the public and private sectors to make the best use of these extraordinary resources. Three examples are citizen education and the maintenance of public space; tourist taxation and after-visit marketing; and the collection of data about quality of life from residents as this relates to consequent action by utility companies.

But all of this is only made possible if there is a widespread urban culture, from basic schooling to economic operators (not only hoteliers and restaurateurs, but also other commercial businesses—and first and foremost public employees). Achieving this is a necessary challenge for Italian cities, and those elsewhere in Europe. It is only if they address this challenge that they will be able to regain their own identities. As Orhan Pamuk has written, for centuries people have looked to Western cities as a model, and now there is a sense of weariness and sadness in old Europe.[4]

Here are cities that for months, for years, for decades have been beloved by their inhabitants. I am thinking in Italy of the emblematic case

---

[3] Joseph Rykwert, *The Seduction of Place* (New York: Pantheon Books, 2000).

[4] Orhan Pamuk, *İstanbul: hatiralar ve şehir* (İstanbul: YKY, 2003); translated as *Istanbul. Memories and the City* (New York: Knopf, 2005).

of Milan, a city for years loved and then for a long time snubbed, almost forgotten as a cultural and architectural treasure, because the ruling classes had forgotten about the city—indeed, regarded it as justifying their own interests regardless of the genius loci. The same could be said of Bilbao, whose strength lies not just in the icon of the Guggenheim, but in the vigor that one feels when one walks its streets, enters any store, enjoys freshly cooked tapas. There is a very close relationship between the city's being and its identity, and for this to be fully expressed, it was necessary for the capital of the Basque region to transform itself.

Cultural attractiveness in Europe

Since 1985, Europe has been pondering how culture can serve to generate urban development and systematize the revitalization of undervalued areas or those in search of new identities. This was first attempted by trying to recover a 19th-century tradition in which architectural heritage was valued, and then in opposing the crisis in Fordism by trying to occupy those spaces that were left empty as economies based on mass production retreated. Gradually, an attitude that had developed in Britain—clear examples of this approach being Glasgow, Bristol, and Liverpool—became mainstream owing to the successful reinvention of Berlin. It became clear that these opportunities were real, and not so much about public sector investment in cultural offerings; rather, and more importantly, they were about attracting young, dynamic, and innovative talent to live at low cost in large urban centers, thus enabling their socioeconomic redevelopment.

It was in 1985 that the then Greek minister of culture, Melina Mercouri, proposed the establishment of an annual "European City of Culture"; this later became "European Capital of Culture." The title was initially given not to specific projects but to cities that were clearly the cultural heart of Europe, such as Athens, Florence, and Weimar. Over the years, the brand has grown stronger until it has become, along with the Erasmus project, one of the Commission's best-known, most coveted, and most talked-about projects, transforming into a competition in which the major cities of a single state participate. The evaluation categories are emblematic and twofold: the offer of cultural innovation produced for and by the citizens who inhabit a particular city, and the ability to give that offering a fully European dimension.

These two themes are central to a helpful definition of cultural attractiveness: something that makes the inhabitants of an area proud and active, that multiplies their skills, that makes them more competitive through an ever-increasing distribution of knowledge; and also something that convinces those who do not live in that particular city or region to visit it, for personal education or for pleasure. This develops into conscious tourist consumption, and eventually individuals or companies are persuaded that a place is so interesting that relocation—whether of a family or a company headquarters—is a judicious move.

Now, almost forty years since Mercouri's initiative was proposed, the situation in many Italian cities has stabilized: There are fewer and fewer cheap areas suitable for redevelopment, fewer and fewer works of art available to be acquired cheaply for display; and there is more and more competition for tourists. Business sectors in neighboring cities act aggressively, reminding us—for better or worse—of what happened in the fourteenth to sixteenth centuries: As mayors are transformed into princes and merchants develop into industrial tycoons, they renovate public spaces and repurpose them as art galleries, disproportionately enhancing the offer that appeals to an increasingly elderly and culturally literate European population. Since 2000, the percentage of tourists who actively choose their destinations for cultural reasons has increased from 25 to 35 percent, while mass media is also benefiting enormously from potential cultural content.

The system of cities and that of regions

In recent years, European urban projects have stood out from regional or macroregional initiatives; there are few success stories in larger areas. A memorable example is the Ruhr, in Germany, which is linked to a diffuse urbanism but above all to a traditional economic system that is collapsing and in need of complete reinvention. In Italy, too, although European programs have viewed the regions as a driving force, it can be argued that only Puglia has, through support for the arts and cultural enterprises, created a brand that has a unified identity, rather than being the sum of individual urban identities.

Projects in Lombardy have evidently been driven by Milan, just as Piedmont has seen a fruitful intersection between the cultural renaissance of Turin and the extraordinary leading role of the Langhe (and

Alba in particular). In many areas, the latter has pivoted on the Slow Food movement and the phenomenon of a material culture that is anchored in the riches of the earth and specific skills related to them—leading to the birth of the University of Taste in Pollenzo.

Triveneto and Marche have in their own way tried to subvert this trend toward localism; but the influence of Venice in the former case (we will return to this in a moment) and the difficulty of becoming a brand in the face of European competition in the latter has made success difficult. It is no coincidence that a lot was riding in both these regions on a bid to become European Capital of Culture, a title that would fall to an Italian city in 2019 (Matera was the successful candidate). As with Turin and the 2006 Olympics or Milan with the 2015 Expo, and explicitly based on the models of the Barcelona Olympics in 1992 and Hannover World Expo in 2000, the two regions were looking for an unambiguous driver that would attest to their renewed cultural identity: This was anchored in a widespread and unique entrepreneurial fabric, but artistic development and architectural innovations capable of transcending the country's borders were lacking.

Cultural attractiveness in Italy

The goal that Triveneto and Marche had set for themselves was by no means easy to achieve, because Italy—whether by choice or not—seems unable to perceive the contemporary as a cultural asset. It is as if the weight of history keeps us anchored to the ground so we cannot fly. It is not only in cultural infrastructure, of which there are very few examples that are not related to redevelopment, but also in cultural productions, which travel very little beyond national borders. There is very little focus on distribution, given that the offer is always tied to the Italian language; this has less impact in the sectors of opera or design—but in the latter case there is less international impact now than there was in the 1960s and 1970s.

This atrophying of Italian offerings internationally—if we exclude a few surprising cases that may or may not endure, examples being the tenor Andrea Bocelli, Il Volo (who describe their music as "popera"), and the rock band Måneskin—contrasts with a local and microlocal hyperactivism, with hundreds of festivals of literature, music, theater, cinema, and even popular science. If science, thanks to the deleterious effect of Benedetto Croce and his followers, was the Cinderella of Italian culture until the 1990s, this is no longer the case. Remarkable local enthusiasm, blending volunteers and microenterprises, exalts the ephemeral and above all the private, with everyone playing multiple roles, and the overall experience is a whirlwind of fragmented ideas and good intentions that do not give rise to movements or trends.

Bell towers or platforms?

The challenge for cultural development in the coming years is therefore to greatly reduce this complexity, to create large collective projects that local actors can converge on and will attract national and international players from the earliest stages. Cities will have to compete less and cooperate more, even if laws and bureaucracies continue to make it difficult for them to achieve their goals.

This, however, does not exclude working voluntarily towards joint goals, based on the commitment not only of cultural institutions but also and especially of citizens, in a direct and unmediated way, and fostered by the use of digital tools. Many examples of this already exist, with good practices spreading at great speed; but they are still too often overwhelmed by traditional procedures. This is not the place to discuss values and truths in communication, but it can be observed that opinions trump quality, especially in culture, and even the most experienced consumer can get lost amid an overwhelming variety of options.

Symbols and idols

To provide an attractive option, you have to decide on your target audience. This is a platitude, but it is worth repeating. You also need to have models and symbols to put forward.

Let us look at Italy and the case of the exceptional development of the Triveneto between 1980 and the 2000s. Venice has the potential to represent an extraordinary opportunity for the region, but it is unfortunately not a good example, to the extent that I will take the liberty of excluding it from the discussion here. In my view, it deserves to be a national priority—on the same level as Naples (however blasphemous this statement may appear). For the rest of the Triveneto, however, culture is a sensitive issue.

Observing the region from the outside, it appears that the general opinion is that there is too much culture of all kinds in Venice and too little elsewhere, meaning that it is unable to take root in families or businesses, let alone in institutions. I don't think this is true, but it is a possibility—even though, in recent times, there have been various actions put in train that disprove this widespread opinion. I will mention only two of them: the redevelopment of the Botanical Garden of Padua and of MUSE, the Science Museum of Trento, which replaced the former Natural Science Museum in 2013. Both have revitalized the area's scientific credentials, and have excellent research groups behind them: Although it often receives little attention, the second aspect is far more relevant than the first. At present, neither the Botanical Garden nor MUSE seems to have become the focus of a new collective identity. They provide additional identities, but they fail to undermine the idea that there is an overpowering material heritage. This problem is national, but particularly evident in the Triveneto.

Intangible heritage

Attractiveness is even more important for intangible heritage than it is for the tangible. It is not large exhibitions that convince someone to move from somewhere else in the world to Italy, not even to an Italy of great beauty such as the Triveneto where this beauty is combined with managerial ability. Rather, it is a matter of focusing on spreading knowledge of Italian skills in the worlds of science, design, and robotics; of imagining how to emphasize the statement repeatedly emphasized by the creative entrepreneur Cristiano Seganfreddo: culture in business, business for culture. We should no longer limit ourselves to the creation of excellent products in a periurban space that hides them away, but rather transfer knowledge horizontally to the community. This is a matter of beginning with training models and widening their application, as has happened with some recent H-FARM proposals. One practice that has spread in the last decade is that of "coderdojo," in which young people work together on technological innovation by designing machine-language responses to specific territorial needs. Another is the cocreation of theatrical and artistic experiences with older people, who are the center of communities in terms of their knowledge of tradition and also want to be involved in community life again. The dancer and choreographer Virgilio Sieni works very diligently on productions of this kind.

Identity, pride, trust

Collective cultural work that puts both younger and older people at its heart gives confidence to a community as it rediscovers its identity; culture becomes a glue that binds people together rather than being a sideshow alongside socioeconomic life. At a time in history when it is finally clear that enrichment should be focused on the spiritual rather than the actual, being a community, thinking about values, and actively pursuing writing, theater, and music brings together a fragmented multiplicity of subjects that have relevance to the future. A utopian aim? It may be. But in the Triveneto, as in the rest of Italy, it is becoming apparent that it is precisely these new relationships that are a road that should be taken with conviction. Putting together this theme of paths with that of technological innovation, while also improving relations with the Eastern Adriatic area and with the Austrian and Hungarian cultural space, the macroregion can be enlarged until it becomes fully European—and relationships within it can be intensified and mutually strengthened.

Italo Calvino writes in *Marcovaldo*:

> For eleven months of the year the inhabitants loved their city and woe to anyone who cast aspersions: the skyscrapers, the cigarette machines, the wide-screen movie theaters, all undeniable sources of constant attraction. [...] At a certain point in the year, the month of August began. And then you witnessed a general change of feeling. Nobody loved the city anymore: even the skyscrapers and the pedestrian subways and the car-parks, till yesterday so cherished, had become disagreeable and tiresome. The inhabitants wanted only to get away as quickly as possible: and so, filling trains and clogging superhighways, by the 15th of the month all of them were actually gone.[5]

This captures it precisely: There can be no more Augusts for cities. They must and can be alive and vibrant 365 days a year and twenty-four hours a day, not only thanks to nightlife but especially thanks to innovation in home automation, which can help us to keep open spaces for production and research in the cultural sphere.

---

[5] Italo Calvino, *Marcovaldo* (London: Secker and Warburg, 1983).

From smart city to smart community: why rebuild cities all together

To get to this point, we need to seriously implement "smart city" projects, but even more so "smart citizenship." We have been talking about smart cities for more than two decades now, but the expression became more important, as it always does, when investment came into play.

Originally, references were to "digital city" and to a greater extent "smart city," but soon an all-technological or technocratic definition became insufficient. A smart city is a city that is not only capable of meeting the challenges of the future but is also, and above all, capable of doing so with a smile on its face, bringing together technology and culture, the skills of the individual, and public policies that are focused on the major problems of daily life. This is not a trivial topic, given that only a few years ago more than half of the world's population lived in cities, and by 2050 this figure will rise to 75 percent, with a monthly increase between now (2022) and then of 5 million people. This is why in Italy, as throughout Europe in recent years, people have stopped betting (all too abruptly, perhaps, at least for companies in the sector) on the existing model for urban expansion and have begun to reflect on improving the lives of citizens through technological innovation. In the first half of the 2010s, this led to a desire to invest more than a billion euro in technological innovation projects in all the main regions of Italy, in a single year. This acceleration was endorsed by the then Minister of Education, University, and Research Francesco Profumo (in office from November 2011 to April 2013) and was implemented by his advisor Mario Calderini.

But when is a city "smart"? And what does it have to do if it wants to go down that road?

There are many ways in which the living conditions of those in an urban area can be improved, especially if that area is very large and very connected. Roads are often clogged, and rush-hour traffic can make urban centers and linking streets unlivable. Starting at the beginning of the new millennium, it became clear to everyone that the traffic problem brings many other failures: too many cars, too many cars with only a single occupant, too much spending on oil, the skyrocketing cost of gasoline, reduced reserves in oil wells, and above all a huge growth in what we have long called the "greenhouse effect," with obvious and tangible global overheating and climate change, and immediate effects on all continents. Reflecting on cities and on their importance to development, given their weight in the distribution of world population, wealth, research, entertainment, and culture, means reflecting on the future of the world. Changing lifestyles in cities mean that new forms of society need to be imagined, with a different role for the management of goods (with the consequent enlargement of the so-called commons and the emergence of the concept, an alternative to that of ownership, of sharing). Being a smart city means providing many cars for co-ownership, having many bicycles for sharing, accepting new schedules for loading and unloading goods, enlarging pedestrian areas, building safe routes for those who go to school without family members necessarily having to be present—even in the case of children attending primary school (and with the use of amusing terms to signal such practices, such as the "*pedibus*," a Latin neologism to indicate walking as a group).

Such actions are almost never the responsibility of administrations alone but are above all reliant on the actions of citizens. A "smart city" does not exist without a "smart community," and this is perhaps the most important and innovative concept of recent years.

Along with the issue of mobility, at the center of the agenda is the question of the planet's resources, which are increasingly scarce in the face of a world population that has reached 7.5 billion people, with fifty new urban areas of more than 10 million inhabitants each in Asia alone, the real protagonist of the current century. As this scenario plays out, new behaviors in relation to the issues of waste, consumption of water, land, and agricultural products are urgently required. A smart community, that is, a community of people who consciously make life choices based on intelligent consumption and management of their time, space, and money, considering all these goods to be of not only individual but also collective relevance, is able to predict its own development and make it sustainable. How is this possible? By making collective choices that are oriented to a broad concept of sustainability, while also being open to dramatic innovation.

One of the main themes here is education, including lifelong learning, and the emergence of a so-called creative class, to use the expression coined by Richard Florida at the time when people were beginning to talk about "smart cities." A city is an engine of development if it brings together science and culture, tradition and innovation to offer new ideas to the whole world, rather than being based on traditional economic forms.

This development has been the only option for many European cities, especially for the so-called Fordist cities, those that had (and in most cases still have) a very strong manufacturing tradition, with more than 50 percent of employment tied to the factories that came into being in the late nineteenth and early twentieth centuries. With the gradual shift of production to the East, and especially with the energy crises in the first half of the 1970s, Western urban centers such as Pittsburgh and Cleveland in the United States, Manchester and Glasgow in the United Kingdom, Cologne in Germany, Lyon in France, and Turin in Italy had to completely rethink their way of being. Indeed, they were all in danger of going the way of Detroit, of losing more than half of the population they had too quickly acquired; but instead they have been able to rise again—some by focusing on biotechnology and medicine (Pittsburgh and Lyon), some on culture (Glasgow and Turin), some on trade fairs (Cologne). Manufacturing has not disappeared in these places but has taken on a new role: Ideas are prototyped, and work is done on design.

In the smart city, speed and quality go hand in hand. Fast connections, especially broadband, are needed to transmit ideas that may be relevant for only a few months but if made available immediately to world markets can produce dramatic returns in a short time. However, this speed of connection does not negate experiences that are defined by a more leisurely approach, such as the slow food movement, which are integrated with quality of life measures in today's cities. Eating selected and seasonal foods offered by a short chain of local producers has become just as smart as walking or biking, sorting garbage, and resorting to video conferencing to exchange information and content, instead of undertaking unnecessary travel. All these aspects have combined in the so-called fifteen-minute city model, an effective metaphor but one that needs to be explored further to discover how it will affect the smooth functioning of both small and large cities.

There remains no doubt that being a smart community means making the best use of contemporary talents and foregrounding good practice.

Events: a word that should be used with care

The word "events" is widely employed today, but is no longer used in its authentic sense: It has taken on negative connotations. Humankind has always needed unique moments, reflections, opportunities for confrontation and encounter; mythical moments on which a community can focus, thereby identifying its myths, exalting them, and then destroying them. This has been happening for more than 10,000 years all over our small planet. Today, the media have reinforced but also fragmented this function. As great scholars such as Edgar Morin, Jean Baudrillard, and Umberto Eco have written, and as Gianfranco Betterini and his research team at the Catholic University of Milan analyzed in depth in the 1980s, first television and then social media (at that time embryonically, but today almost universally) have mixed up the quotidian moments of daily life and celebratory occasions. Erving Goffman has spoken of a social revolution, one that has changed the very concept of the week, and of the day. We have new rhythms now, and we have to take this into account. Those who marvel at the success of Expo 2015 in Milan seem to have failed to understand that there is still an absolute need to gather in a place with something we can all share and talk about, to get together and have fun, to not always be serious or self-destructive, but to rejoice instead.

For me, perceiving events in an appropriate context means recognizing people's happiness and joy. Rarely have I seen people as happy as during the first white night of the Winter Olympics in Turin or at the opening of Expo 2015 or when the city of Matera was named European Capital of Culture in 2019. These are unique moments in the history of cities, and in the West they can dictate a city's rhythms. Indeed, events such as those I have mentioned are by no means exceptional or unique; rather, they are cyclical. The community needs them to occur regularly so as to dictate the rhythms of life. Sometimes they happen at the right moments, in step with social, political, and economic developments; sometimes they are not opportune, and the community rejects them if they are not stopped in time. But one cannot be for or against events of this kind regardless of the overall situation. There have always been (and will continue to be) major events that obscure humanitarian disasters, reminding us of the great evils that are possible in society: Think, for example, of the 1978 World Cup in Argentina, before which the recently installed military junta was accused of "disappearing" over 5500 of the country's citizens. But, in contrast, without the 1992 Barcelona Olympics, I believe we would not have had a generation of European citizens. That event dictated the urban rhythms not only of Spain but also of all old Europe for almost two decades.

The fatigue around making choices is always there, even in major events; but having a date that must be adhered to in an absolute and unmissable way is hugely advantageous, especially in democracies. Because a fixed date acts as a regulating element; it forces decisions. If decisions are made well and quickly, with a high standard of collective decision-making and organization, events will be of a higher quality. Anglo-Saxon countries seem to do this by default, and "use" events better; while Latin countries demonstrate a greater need for a more orderly approach.

It should be enough to start early and with the right aims, without trying to slip in unrelated issues under cover of major events. One might, for example, choose to merge a range of infrastructure policies, but it is essential to be as clear as possible about the scenario in which the choices and possibilities for community growth are taking shape. Raise the bar but not too high, otherwise the community will revolt. And engage the community in an orderly manner, so it grows in step with its administrators. An event should serve to make people proud of their area, understanding the opportunities and also the limitations. There is no single way in which to do this. All depends on the needs of the community, and the ability of local leaders to read opportunities for development.

Generally, the major issues at stake are always the same: infrastructure, training, innovation, enterprise, culture, sustainability. But what should an urban agenda be for? To create a city that functions in a conventional manner? Or (also) to dictate medium- to long-term development? And how do these two elements come together?

Every community must be able to express its aspirations. Today, the European urban agenda seems to be obsessed with the issue of jobs. Quite right. But perhaps we should be even more attentive to societal models. We are changing, and the pandemic has highlighted this. It is the new aspirations, the new utopias that must dictate progress. Some changes may be destructive—just as putting up new walls and building defensive citadels was initially in the medieval period. But events, the big ones, the real ones, always require us to overcome barriers and boundaries. That's another of their strengths!

Innovation is always possible, and major events are a great test as well as a catalyst for change. It is not a question of size, although of course there is a great difference between holding a World Expo and being appointed a European Capital of Culture. The former has a definite bounded physicality dictated by the Bureau International des Expositions; the latter can use sites that are already available without any new spaces being built at all. But what I would like to point out here is how many kinds of innovation can be brought to bear: technological, social, political, economic. To innovate is not just to open up new routes to development, but to rethink the society in which you live.

As an example, this has been the challenge of Matera 2019: to build a new local thinking that is capable of anticipating the challenges of the future rather than merely submitting to them. In this specific case, the size of the city created conflicting and almost paradoxical elements: It was very large in area but with a low number of inhabitants per square kilometer. Matera was a perfect venue for experimentation, as there were very diverse audiences in terms of ages, skills, and basic ideas. But it also had a not insignificant problem: few public administration employees who were ready to accept the challenge. Ordinary citizens were much more willing to participate. This is why we decided, before we got to content production, to work on training: This was detailed in the application dossier, and was widely acclaimed by the judging committee. This goal was divided into three main areas: 1) content production; 2) broadening audiences and strengthening their skills; and 3) running courses to improve the operational standards of municipal and regional staff, what we termed creative bureaucracy. In hindsight, these three elements are not only a textbook model for the events sector and for cities seeking revitalization, but are important for organizations at national and supranational levels. All these aspects are now intertwined with the ubiquitous dimensions of smart working and distance learning.

In the case of Expo 2015, the aims of the event were also quantitative: many different nations from all continents exhibiting on a properly equipped site; raising awareness of the proposed theme ("Feeding the Planet, Energy for Life") among a huge number of spectators; handling an impressive flow of goods; bringing heads of state and ministers to Italy; welcoming many schoolchildren to the pavilions; putting research centers to work; and much more. Milan won the bid, properly interpreting the theme and performing a second Italian miracle after the 2006 Winter Olympics in Turin (a smaller event in terms of impact and numbers, and in a more manageable city). Expo 2015 did not cause memorable traffic jams; the subway worked well, as did the parking lots and entrance procedures. One can argue about the quality and rigor of individual exhibitors, but the theme was handled well by at least twenty out of the fifty-four pavilions, being discussed in the media to a tedious extent and stimulating thousands of on-site and off-site debates. It cannot be said that the rules of the Bureau International des Expositions were ignored; quite the contrary. In Shanghai, one might argue that the inhabitants of an entire subcontinent were forced to visit the Expo in 2010; in Italy and Europe, this was not the case. Some turned their noses up at it, saying that people only visited "because everyone else was going," that Expo was primarily a media event, and was nothing remarkable. No Expo has changed the history of the world, but a few have certainly marked a turning point in a particular area of development: For the Milanese, this was certainly the case for their Expo dedicated to the theme of nutrition.

If we look at urban infrastructure, even though Expo 2015 took place in one of Italy's densest metropolitan areas, the legacy is there today: On the one hand, there is the new purple metro line; on the other hand, the redevelopment of the Darsena waterfront, the first step in the restoration of the Navigli area. This is not to mention the focus on private investment thanks to Expo. The importance acquired by the area that pivots around the Porta Garibaldi station and Piazza Gae Aulenti, Milan's most modern neighborhood; the new Fondazione Prada headquarters in the former industrial area centered on the Porta Romana railway yard; the Mostrami factory @Folli 50.0 project, an "art yard, aggregation space" that is being promoted by Fondazione Bracco in the historic industrial area in the Lambrate district: These are just a few examples of redevelopment that arouses great admiration outside Italy.

It must be said that Expo 2015 was lucky too. After several years that were much less encouraging, Italy experienced a memorable summer, with increased tourist numbers—largely benefiting from the crisis in Egypt, Tunisia, Turkey, and even Greece. But being lucky is not a fault; on the contrary. And Expo 2015 set the stage for a historic opportunity that the country can still ride, alongside a study of new tourism mechanisms that are better suited to contemporary times.

Two other points about Expo 2015's success should also be mentioned. Without a doubt, the event revitalized Milan, which has responded with dedication to the cause after an initial, inevitable, skepticism. But what I regard as the most important aspect concerns Italy as a whole; in other words, Expo's connection with the rest of the country. As an emblematic figure who played an important role in Expo 2015, Giacomo Biraghi, founder of the #expottimists movement, said, Expo was "hacked." What does that mean?

I take Biraghi's comment as suggesting that everyone has been able to use the event as a tool to highlight his or her own qualities. On the penultimate day of Expo, after three years of promoting it, I was invited to Buronzo, a small town in the province of Vercelli, with about a thousand inhabitants and a thousand years of history. On the occasion of the Expo, four exhibitions were set up in Buronzo's castle, using resources made available by Piedmontese banking foundations, and the small town was made one of the three displays of the territorial system "Strada del Riso Vercellese di Qualità," receiving visits from hundreds of entrepreneurs in the rice sector and more than 10,000 tourists. On October 30, 2015, a large rice mandala was made by twenty young people of all ages and backgrounds, and this was commented upon by four representatives of monotheistic religions (Buddhism, Christianity, Judaism, Islam) in the presence of the whole village, who expressed their pride in being part of the Expo system. This local pride, this eagerness to take up a position within the framework of something bigger and shared, is I believe a great and unquestionable success of Expo 2015.

If Expo 2015 marked a very important moment for the country at a global level, Matera's appointment as European Capital of Culture in 2019 made it clear that it is not only the North that can host prestigious events, but also that even smaller urban realities, seemingly far from everywhere, can take on and win an equal challenge. It was well known that the European Commission had set its sights on the city of Lucania in order to revive an initiative that had been one of Europe's greatest successes over the years. But for a long time, perhaps with the exception of Marseille, becoming European Capital of Culture left no trace in the collective memory, did not give rise to new ways of doing things, and left behind almost no significant urban transformations. While Milan succeeded in relaunching the Expo, Matera refreshed the European Capital of Culture event in 2019: This was a hundred times less expensive than the Expo, but potentially of even greater impact in the long run. Already at the candidacy stage, the Italy 2019 coalition impressed Brussels. Fundamental were the concepts of "temporary citizen" (with which Matera wanted to replace the term "tourist") and that of "cultural inhabitant," an evolution and integration of ideas that were applied in Belgium, in Mons, in 2015, and also found a place in Leuwaarden, in the Netherlands, in

2018. But the latter two are cities that have a weight not comparable with that of Matera, which has seen foreign tourism increase by 140 percent and has enjoyed unique international media visibility, with appearances in the *New Yorker*, the *Wall Street Journal*, *Vanguard*, and in dozens of other outlets, as well as gaining a massive online presence.

The success of Milan and Matera encouraged large metropolitan areas to imagine new goals and new investments and smaller towns to feel included in a new project of nationhood, aspiring to new ways of telling their stories and encouraging pride in their localities.

Suddenly all this came to a halt because of the pandemic; but just months after the first lockdown the recovery is touching all areas—and it is precisely the most marginal places that have the greatest chance of revival. The urban challenge has by no means stopped because of COVID-19; on the contrary; it has highlighted more clearly what many urban planners have been emphasizing since 2008. A return to community living, nonconfrontational and with shared goals and tools, was already being strongly called for. This has now become a moral and operational necessity.

A high-speed axis for Italy's development and the lack of a collective strategy

The National Recovery and Resilience Plan; EU funds allocated for 2021–2027; national financial funding; resources made available by the European Investment Bank; funds offered to public and private markets by the most important and proactive banks: Amid all these initiatives, is it possible to discern an overall strategy for Italy's development, starting with the cities? And, if so, which cities? And how?

We know well that the whole of Europe is a complex urban system, as has been stated by Stefano Boeri and reiterated by former European Commission President Jose Manuel Barroso at the symbolic conclusion of his political journey at the head of the Old Continent, when he presented the results of the *New Narratives of Europe* project.[6] We also know

---

[6] Details of *New Narrative for Europe. The Mind and Body of Europe*, the project launched in April 2013, can be downloaded at: https://ec.europa.eu/assets/eac/culture/policy/new-narrative/documents/declaration_en.pdf. On Barroso's

that nearly seven out of ten citizens in Europe live in urban areas, and that the economic and cultural vitality of an area depends on the ability of metropolitan systems to plan for the medium to long term. But in Italy, which along with Germany is the European region in which cities play a predominant role, do we know how to invest in an integrated way using cross-sectoral and cross-regional planning?

Some great opportunities have already been missed, perhaps because we have asked too much of politics and too little of policy. In the last decade, from Turin 2006 to the Milan Expo in 2015, cities in the North took advantage of big events to change their identity and image, doing what Spanish cities had put into practice in the first half of the 1990s. But the same did not happen in the South, especially in Naples, where the Universal Forum of Cultures promoted by UNESCO, which was supposed to take place in 2013 and which, owing to many economic and political woes, was shifted to 2014, was neither an occasion for new development nor for strengthening collective pride.

By contrast, the work done in Turin along the railway axis, with an extraordinary enhancement of the cultural offer, and the private investment that in Milan led to the birth of the new neighborhood of Porta Nuova, on a grand scale and quality, are the fruits of modes of intervention that are quite different from each other and consistent with the historical peculiarities and even social characteristics of the two great urban areas of the North. Turin took on board public urban strategic plans characterized by explicit partnerships, of the type that were inaugurated by the Lyon administration, continued by Glasgow, and established in the experiences of Barcelona and Bilbao. In Milan, there was investment by private individuals, lively deregulation, and an international influence. In both localities, urban elites reflected on the ongoing crisis, the transition from the Fordist to the post-Fordist city, and the necessary relationships between education and innovation. For a long time, Milan had been much more capable of grasping contemporary challenges; but at the end of the 1990s, Turin was able to stave off for a while the fear of the loss of FIAT as the city's sole economic star, thanks to a new idea of a "bright" city that would counter the widespread grayness of the 1970s and 1980s.

Those were the years when a third, more central, Po Valley star shone:

---

speech on March 1, 2014, see "Imagining Europe as a big city, Barroso takes up Boeri's idea," https://www.adnkronos.com/, March 1, 2014.

Bologna. This star suddenly dimmed in the 1990s, at a time when Rome and Naples were finally gaining investments in culture and education. An interesting focus on infrastructure in Naples and an initial timid outing into the world of new architecture in Rome were unable, however, to bring to fruition a thoughtful and lasting path for urban renewal.

A history of urban transformation in Italy could be very detailed, but perhaps this is not the place for such an extensive chronicle. However, a table on investments and returns derived from urban transformations of all kinds would clearly show what has happened in the last twenty years and what could—and perhaps should—happen in the next twenty. What is certain is that all the cities referred to so far are aligned along a single route thanks to one network entity: the State Railways. While port, airport, trade fair, and university policies have seen fierce competition and produced considerable and often deleterious fragmentation (in the vain hope that competition between banking foundations could bring about a new Renaissance), the choices that have been made to impose the Frecciarossa high speed trains as Italy's developmental axis are without a shadow of a doubt the most important of the last quarter century. It is a pity that this development has been internal, and so far has had no strong ramifications for France, Germany, or Austria. This should be urgently addressed. What is certain is that the Frecciarossa axis has produced a strong integration between Turin and Milan, Bologna and Florence, Rome and Naples, almost creating new urban bipolarities—something that the talented Richard Florida noticed as early as 2009 in *Who's Your City?*[7]

Outside this axis, meanwhile, new urban strategies have been imposed. The Tyrrhenian area of the North brings together the ancient maritime republics of Genoa and Pisa, which always had the potential for expansion but were never sufficiently assisted by national and regional systems; the birth of a unified logistics hub should also include La Spezia and Livorno. There is also a double pole to the northeast of Milan, represented on the one hand by the powerful areas of Bergamo and Brescia, which are capable of empowering each other, through the Trentino-Alto Adige region, and on the other hand by the Veneto pole that seeks to become a network-city on the Dutch model, but so far has not fully succeeded. On

---

[7] Richard Florida, *Who's Your City?: How the Creative Economy Is Making Where You Live the Most Important Decision of Your Life* (New York: Basic Books, 2008).

the eastern side of the country there are also two major question marks, Trieste and Venice, which are in demographic and also planning decline.

In the South, meanwhile, some small- to medium-sized cities (of which about 70 percent of Europe's urban fabric is composed) are trying to raise their profiles again and set themselves up as models that are successfully responding to new challenges through the use of unprecedented social and cultural models. This is the case for Matera and potentially for Taranto. Let us remember that south of Rome there is only 12 percent of Italy's cultural product and just under 15 percent of the country's international tourism (despite Puglia's popularity and wider European and non-European love for the Amalfi coast and some Sicilian destinations). There is no real banking presence, and the seasonality of tourism causes much wage instability.

The relationship between these cities and their related opportunities is still constrained by administrative arrangements that are totally inadequate for attracting foreign investment at a time when the international resources available are very significant. Governmental discussions about risk are blocking potential urban development. Since 1994, there has not been a Department of Urban Areas in Italy, and there is not even an online map using open data to show the primary urban transformation projects underway, either in Italian or in English. Mayors are seeing their responsibilities increase and their resources decrease; while the Delrio law (Law No. 56 of April 7, 2014), which extended the perimeter of metropolitan areas, has not resulted in growing awareness of what a metropolitan area is or shown how a true supramunicipal instrument can bring enormous benefits—see in France the case of Grand Lyon. The open filing of investment opportunities and a constant exchange of information between actors who have similar interests could help to create a collective strategy that would be capable of bringing public and private interests together.

Lessons learned from around the world

There is nothing more exciting than going around the world to hear about urban development projects. Anyone working in city government, large or small, should go to MIPIM in Cannes, the great real estate investment fair, at least once: The event offers the largest annual overview of potential and ongoing urban transformations. Having worked for the World Bank on the creation of the Rio de Janeiro metropolitan area (in 2014) and having been invited a few months later by Moscow's Skolkovo University to speak with the mayors of Russia's thirty most important monograds (those cities born under Stalin with the purpose of being productive districts dominated by a single industry or company, on the model of Turin), I can testify that the questions raised by administrators and experts are really very similar all around the world. I lack the experience of working in a large African city, such as Lagos or Nairobi, but I have seen with my own eyes the doubling in size of the city of Cairo, thanks to two satellite new towns that are being built just outside Giza.

The COVID-19 pandemic, far from reducing the role of cities in terms of global development, has thrown down the challenge of rethinking them to make them safer from a health standpoint, pushing for ever greater use of open spaces, with life moving from schools and offices to public squares (covered or not), and with new places to study, work, and have fun. But the pandemic has also made us realize—with more force than any scientific essay, protest, or collective communication—that over the next twenty-five years we will face three major challenges that will touch all of us as citizens:

- *Learning to cooperate*, even before we think about competing. Cities, and society more generally, will succeed if integration is pursued, rather than different models being pitted against each other. Dutch as well as Austrian cities are among those that have best understood how to bring development and sustainability together with a great sense of collective responsibility.
- *Rebalancing the relationship between nature and culture*. The role of natural areas will once again have a greater weight than built-up areas. During lockdowns, images of animals in deserted cities quickly reclaiming the spaces they had lost went around the world. The animal kingdom must become the basis of a new thinking about the relationship between citizens and the rest of the cosmos, starting with inland and mountain areas.
- *Regulate the clash between real and digital*. Cities will be the main scene of this new opportunity. We will be called upon to avoid all forms of technological "slavery" and to make the best use of our time in properly designed urban spaces. Pedestrian areas, electric

> mobility, study places that can become business spaces: Our cities need to be rethought, taking into account new skills and new flexibility.

The 21st century may indeed be the "urban century." But the protagonists will have to be the citizens, not the cities themselves. For this to happen, key words will have to be spread not only among *urban practitioners* but also to all urban dwellers in the next decade: These words are confidence and courage. Confidence in a society that we perceive to be increasingly polarized and in which we must work to reduce fragmentation without losing sight of individuals' values. Courage in making choices, in seeking priorities, in sharing them with citizens and individual interest groups. The same confidence and courage that are the real protagonists of the nine city stories you are about to read.

1 Barcelona
From dictatorship to autonomy

An open city

"Barcelona is an open city, and from this moment on it is your city." These words, addressed to everyone on the planet, were uttered in English by the city's mayor, Pasqual Maragall, on July 25, 1992, during the opening ceremony of the twenty-fifth Summer Olympics. They were more than a statement; they were the expression of a real political program that had been realized in ten years and was a bridge to the following decade.

Candidature for the twenty-fifth Olympic Games was put forward in 1981, only two years after the first democratic elections in Spain. At that time, local authorities had very few economic resources and were having to deal with urban problems inherited from decades of dictatorship.

Handing the microphone to Juan Antonio Samaranch, president of the International Olympic Committee (IOC), Maragall brought the model of the new city of the 21st century to over 3.5 billion television viewers worldwide, an achievement that was well ahead of its time. From being an industrial city that grew up in the shadow of the Franco dictatorship, with its sea front obstructed by the railway and disconnected from main trade and tourism routes, Barcelona had managed to close every gap between it and other cities in the ten years that Maragall's socialist administration had been in charge, with a determination to change that made it a world model. At the end of the 20th century, every mayor in the world wanted a future for his city that mirrored Barcelona's success.

Few are aware that this powerful visionary capacity had only recently been channeled into structured governance: The city's strategic plan was born in 1990, aimed at selecting priorities collectively and consciously, and—above all—to involve certain actors as promoters of change. Thirty years of strategic planning have followed, with the elaboration of five strategic plans; the first three were at municipal level and the last two on a metropolitan scale.

According to the definition proposed by Termcat, the Catalan linguistic center, reported on the website of the Barcelona Metropolitan Strategic Plan, "A strategic plan contains in a detailed and systematic form the objectives of an organization [or area development], the policies and actions planned to achieve them in a given period, and the corresponding control systems and instruments."[1]

Barcelona's first strategic plan, developed between 1990 and 1994, aimed to consolidate the city as a European metropolis, configuring it as the center of a European macroregion, primarily by improving quality of life and strengthening industry and advanced business services.

At the same time, the Association for the Strategic Plan, formally founded in 1989 (but not active until the following year), began its work on elaborating the city's first strategic plan. This private, nonprofit organization brings together the thirty-six municipalities that make up the Metropolitan Area of Barcelona, the Autonomous Region of Catalonia, the Provincial Council of Barcelona, the Association of Municipalities of the Metropolitan Area of Barcelona (Mancomunitat de Municipis), the Chamber of Commerce, the Cercle d'Economia, the Employment Promotion Agency (Foment del Treball), the University of Barcelona, the Fira de Barcelona, the metropolitan transport system, and environment governing bodies, the Barcelona Port Authority and Barcelona-El Prat Airport, and trade union representatives.

Crisis

Before coming up with strategies, Barcelona had experienced moments of great difficulty; it is difficult now to imagine what it must have been like in the 1970s for a city that is so well known today: It was in the grip of an industrial crisis from which it could not extricate itself, had been subjugated by the undemocratic Francoist power based in Madrid,

---

[1] See "Barcelona Vision 2020." https://pemb.cat/.

and was symbolized by the Barrio Gotico district as a place of ill-favor and housing poverty. The crisis of the 1970s had bequeathed the city an economic model that was based on manufacturing industry, a model that had reached its limits and needed serious change. But the crisis also coincided with the birth of the new Spain and its entry into the European Union.

This was an extraordinary opportunity that Maragall, reelected as mayor for the third time, was able to seize not only by nominating the city to host the Olympic Games, but also by imagining the occasion as a moment of extraordinary transformation of the city's economic and social structure. Many point out that this happened inclusively: All social groups were engaged in the bid to build a more beautiful, livable, and attractive city. This development sat behind a new welfare model, one that saw the birth of a widespread middle class, a real new urban bourgeoisie, made up of young people who were able to put into practice theories about the knowledge society and creativity.

Relaunch

Sport as an engine for change: not just the Olympics

In October 1986, when Barcelona was confirmed as the venue for the Olympic Games, it was realized that this was the perfect opportunity to find the necessary resources for the transformation the city had been waiting for. This is why the 1992 Olympics certainly represent not only the most important example of urban transformation in the last thirty years, but also the perfect testimony of how one can take advantage of events of international importance to modify and improve public spaces.

The Catalan city decided to capitalize on the stimulus provided by the IOC not only to redevelop large parts of the city—from Montjuic, which was in a complete state of disrepair and in need of extensive renovation to accommodate the main sports facilities, to the aforementioned Barrio Gotico and, obviously, the entire coastline, which before 1992 had only one small beach, Barceloneta—but also, and above all, to give a new role to the inhabitants; to foreground their pride, their identity. Montjuic had already been transformed for the Universal Exhibition of 1929, the last major international event that the city had hosted before the Second

World War—so it was not just a matter of reconstruction, but of bringing the city back to life.

As many of those directly involved have repeatedly stated, it was necessary to act simultaneously on three fronts: to create jobs, decentralize management functions, and stimulate cooperation between the public and private sectors. All in all, the private sector invested more than 3 billion euro, compared with more than 6 billion from the public sector, including municipal, regional, and ministerial resources, and also state-owned companies.

The role of sport as a considerable influence on social cohesion and cultural integration should also be emphasized: It is no coincidence that the then councilor for sport, Enric Truno, had been councilor for the education system in previous legislatures, with a particular interest in making the younger generations the engine of change. Barcelona was the first city to decide to provide a sports space in every neighborhood, as well as an educational and cultural space—a project that was carefully studied by London in 2012 and led to the United Kingdom not only locating centers of sports promotion and excellence in the capital, but also throughout the nation (examples being those dedicated to swimming and diving, to athletics, and to rowing).

A particularly emblematic role was played by the construction of the athletes' village, the so-called Vila Olímpica del Poblenou, on the coast, where there had only been railways and decaying 19th-century industries. This structure was necessary to accommodate the more than 12,000 athletes who would come from all over the world: The space it occupied, which until then had been perceived as outside the historical city, was completely returned to use by everyone—to the citizens before the tourists. The Vila Olímpica, today one of the postcard images of the city, received investments totaling 2 billion euro for the construction of flats to house the athletes. The other neighborhoods in which urban works were concentrated were Vall d'Hebron, until then a free space, which was converted into an urban park, with sports facilities of lesser importance; and Avinguda Diagonal, where pavements and pedestrian areas were widened, and where the center for journalists was built.

The development of these different locations also necessitated a new transport plan. There was considerable investment in the road system, but above all in large infrastructure such as the airport, which over the decades has played a decisive role in the growth of both leisure and business tourism: There were 7 million users in 1990 and over 50 million in 2019. The problem of a lack of capacity in the hotel sector also had to be faced: Barcelona was not yet on the circuit of cities famous for their art and culture; on the contrary, attracting visitors represented a real innovation. At first, the hotels thought they could easily cope with the increased demand during the fortnight of the Olympics by charging exorbitant prices to customers staying in the city and diverting everyone else to hotels on the Costa Brava. However, with the support of the government, the sector realized that a new era was beginning for the hotel industry. It may seem unbelievable today, but until 1992 tourism generated less than 2 percent of Barcelona's GDP; after the Olympics, and the uninterrupted growth that followed, it has come to generate as much as 15 percent.

Football as an identity metaphor

Alongside the Olympics and the city administration's direct influence, a fundamental role in Barcelona's development has been played by one sport above all: football. Since the year of its foundation in 1899, Futbol Club Barcelona has always been a symbol of the area. The correspondence in growth between the club (a budget of 30 million euro in 1988 and around 900 million euro in 2018) and the city is incredible. After the crisis years of the 1970s and the relative power of Real Madrid, Barcelona FC has seen the growth in value of its brand go hand in hand with that of the city's brand since the return of Johan Crujff to the Blaugrana bench in 1988. Just as Barcelona has become a global city, Barça has become the first global team, loved all over the world and with a capacity for collective identification that was previously reserved for individual champions. Perhaps Crujff himself played a role in this, bringing to Spain the teachings of the great Netherlands teams of 1974 and 1978. The ability to make a team became the core of how the city and its citizens could grow intelligently—until at least 2004.

Stabilization

After the extraordinary success of the Olympics, which immediately made Barcelona not only the most desirable tourist destination for short breaks, but also in some ways the capital of the new Europe—to the extent that Jacques Delors commissioned Maragall to preside over the Council of European Regions and Cities, at a magical moment when individual territories really seemed to be the driving force behind less invasive and less inefficient states—the city realized that it had to work immediately on its relaunch, plan the consolidation of its image; and above all boost its relations with the international economy. This is how the second strategic plan of Barcelona came into being: Between 1994 and 1997, this generated a positive response to the new demands for social integration, while also guaranteeing the performance of new economic activities with a clear expectation of their globalization.

After these results had been consolidated, the third strategic plan was prepared, oriented toward promoting economic, social, and urban transformation between 1999 and 2003, in response to the knowledge society and to consolidate Barcelona's position within national borders and on international markets. But how to make this primacy visible? With what event should the urban transformation initiated in the early 1990s be concluded and the attractiveness for investment, especially foreign investment, be relaunched, given that "local" public and private resources had been drained in the previous decade?

The Forum of Cultures

"The Forum is an opportunity to meet and reflect on the contemporary challenges facing humanity; ambassadors from all the world's cultures will come together for 141 days to discuss issues related to cultural diversity, sustainable development and the necessary conditions for peace." It was Pasqual Maragall, once again, who at the end of his third term as mayor—in 1996—proposed a new event that would consolidate not only Barcelona's role as a leading city for the economy and tourism, but also the idea of a new urban culture, capable of connecting people and building a true and permanent peace between peoples. This utopia was already present in the words of the Catalan politician in his inaugural speech in July 1992: At that time, he had cited the ongoing wars in the former Yugoslavia as an unacceptable state of affairs for the United Nations.

After running for President of the Regional Government, and then founding the European Democratic Party, Maragall, with the group of socialist leaders who shared his vision at a turning point in the history of his city, of Spain, and of Europe, imagined a third world pole, which would take advantage of the fall of the Berlin Wall, of technological innovation that was in its infancy but was clearly an important player, of the spread of Spanish as a fundamental language not only in Latin America, but also among the many new Americans whom the Clinton administration was integrating (particularly those from Mexico), as a sociocultural milieu to which it would offer a stage. Barcelona would provide a space for designing and imagining a new world system, which it would lead. This was to be called the Forum of Cultures: It would allow the city to conclude its transformation process and to enter the new millennium as a protagonist, an urban area in which social inclusion, wellbeing, technology, and tourism merged into a unique urban offer.

For Barcelona, what Francis Fukuyama wrote at the time (also in 1992) seems to apply: Were we at the end of history? At the beginning of an eternal present?

The Forum of Cultures was an idea rather than a physical entity; it was an intelligent proposal that offered a third theme—not the sports of the IOC (based in Lausanne), not the commercial novelties of Expo as represented by the Bureau International des Expositions (based in Paris), but the cultures of the new millennium as the basis for sustainable development. The meeting of peoples and their ideas, which occurs in Barcelona every day with the arrival of millions of tourists, would become an event that lasted more than four months, between the six months of Expo and the three Olympic weeks (plus the two Paralympic weeks). The venue was to be the Poble Nou area, where the city's waste had been piled up until then. Barcelona's landfill became the emblem of a new Renaissance. The metaphor was evident, and even convinced UNESCO—which in 1997 agreed with the city that the new event should be held every three years, with the capital of Catalonia as the first venue, of course.

There were three themes: cultural diversity, sustainable development, conditions for peace. On the sidelines, but the substance of the related urban project, was the birth of a super-connected district, not by chance called 22@ (this reads "22 arroba" and although it looks forward to the 22nd century, it also might remind us a little of Lettera 22, the typewriter that Olivetti made into an icon of the 20th century).

Maragall and his collaborators, among whom the figure of Manuel Castells stood out, sociologist and theorist of networks but also of a new European identity, imagined a space entirely dedicated to creativity, a large temporary theme park. The model was that of Expo, but with greater visitor participation, as they are able to participate in the dozens of discussions and debates organized at the same time as the exhibitions. More than to see, you would visit to do something; and the emblem of the event was the wonderful congress pavilion designed by Herzog & De Meuron.

What struck the visitor immediately was the entrance wall, upon which the names of the cities and regions participating in the discussions were updated daily. Barcelona became a platform for knowledge and thus paid homage to its knowledge-based strategic plan. In addition to importing talent and tourists, and thereby creating widespread industrial and commercial activity, the city exported a model—that of a new civilization based on networking and the ability to plan together for the present and the future in a responsible and collective manner.

The event opened on 9 May 2004. It comprised five large visiting areas, including a camp for 1200 children from all the war zones of the world. Remarkably, this was the same year in which Terra Madre was born in Turin, an event that was initially related to the great success of the Salone del Gusto, but gradually broke away from it to become the most important space for reflection for the world agricultural community. Carlin Petrini, the founder of Slow Food, shared with Maragall the idea of a proactive world, which regarded individual human beings as being responsible for the life of the planet—the most important asset to take care of. The end of the 20th century offered these two projects as symbolizing a single great nation, but the 2001 attacks on the Twin Towers opened a new front of combat: This was no longer in the mountainous territories of Afghanistan, but the war had been brought home, to borrow an expression that Luca Rastello coined for the conflicts in the former Yugoslavia.

In comparison with Terra Madre, the Forum was less rigorous in its choice of business partners, and what the event's planners theoretically hoped for clashed with a new underlying theme: the relationship between cultures of sustainability, ethics, urban capitalism, and multinational investment.

The Forum did not repeat the success of the Olympics for a technical reason: It was not an event for the media, although in the end more journalists were accredited to it than had followed the Games; but it was a major initiative with enormous promotion and management costs in which citizens participated. If the Olympics are the motion of the heart, a gesture of revitalization that we find in Barcelona's Olympic logo (a line of color that becomes a body), the Forum was a highly intellectual act, involving a radical transformation of a specific part of the city. It was not widespread; it was mostly realized with private foreign investment; it was, in every sense, speculative.

The budget for the Forum was over 3 billion euro, which was covered by six public partners and fifteen private sponsors, among whom were new large Catalan and Spanish companies (La Caixa—now Caixabank—the big bank of Catalonia, together with Iberia and Telefonica), but also multinationals such as Coca-Cola and Nestlé, which were in the dock at the time for their economic and management models relating to production and distribution: Their involvement brought strong criticism from the likes of Amnesty International and Greenpeace, who were also among the Forum's intellectual protagonists. For the first time, a movement against the Forum was formed, which caused a dramatic fracture between the social will of the event and the concrete effects on Catalan society.

In reality, 90 percent of the budget was used for the innovative physical transformation of the area redeveloped for the Forum, and only 10 percent for the events, which included 19 exhibitions, 450 live shows, 47 round tables, and 11 themes. While from a physical point of view, unlike the Olympics, everything was centralized in the southeast area of the city, events and shows also took place outside the Forum's enclosure, touching on many other municipalities in the region. This, however, did not shift the general perception of an event that was born more out of urban necessity than collective need. Although everything or almost everything was built with the participation of the associations involved, the Olympic impact was not repeated.

Yet the overall effect was remarkable. Thanks to the Forum, Barcelona became the world's leading conference tourism destination, with a conference center capable of accommodating over 15,000 people, currently the largest in the world. All this was set in a new park, not by chance named Peace Park. Mobility was optimal, not only thanks to the new metro line, but also by virtue of the restoration of the tram that traditionally connected this area to the city center. The plan was so well thought out that it finally allowed completion of the Avinguda Diagonal, one of Barcelona's broadest and most important avenues that had been designed by the engineer and urban planner Ildefons Cerdà more than a hundred years earlier. Sustainability was total: In place of the landfill site, a large square was created, covered by a highly innovative photovoltaic system that produced energy for the new district's infrastructure. The square sat above the sewage treatment plant, which enabled the construction of a second marina connected to new housing developments. Finally, at the center of the new technological district was the Audiovisual Campus: five buildings totaling 60,000 square meters capable of attracting the best national and international multimedia companies. Thanks to the Forum, Barcelona made a bid to be the planet's cultural center, to be its new Athens. Its intellectuals worked hard on this; but the planet shifted on its axis. Barcelona is no longer the capital of the world—because the world is no longer just the West.

Technology parks, innovation, and social inclusion

The development of the new Barcelona in the southeast connected to the Forum of Cultures and the third strategic plan, which had a purely urban dimension but was strongly marked by the development of the knowledge economy, has contributed to the construction of a new urban identity, made up not only of history, architecture, sport, and tourism, but also and above all technological transfer between researchers and enterprises.

Catalunya's first science parks date back to 1999, when the decision was taken to make the region an center for life sciences research, particularly biotechnology. Capable of producing not only knowledge but also quality of life, these parks have had a strong impact on the restructuring of the city's economy, gradually replacing many industrial functions and contributing to the emergence of a stronger service economy: It is estimated that every worker employed in innovation-related sectors generates five other jobs, above all qualified positions in the fields of law, education, and health; this may be compared with the impact of industrial systems, in which every new job brings two others, but in decidedly less profitable sectors. A characteristic that should not be overlooked is that out of the approximately 3000 people employed in the technology parks, 54 percent are women (starting with Maria Terrades, CEO of the Parc Científic de Barcelona from May 17, 2020), and this results in a distinctively female way of thinking.

However, the focus on science parks does not just have positive effects: Workers in this sector have a higher standard of living, so there is a powerful increase in so-called gentrification. In short, talent costs money, even if it carries a message of tolerance, international connections, and new ideas for development. In return, more and more urban services are demanded, and in the long run very visible social differences can be generated. Precisely because Barcelona has become a very attractive city to work in and has been able to create efficient urban ecosystems for particular sectors, other social actors have felt—perhaps not rightly, but very strongly—excluded from the project. The great competition that has been created has produced very strong internal fractures, as well as a more marked demand for autonomy. As in the case of Milan in the 1980s and 1990s, it was from among the wealthier classes, and also the more traditional inhabitants, that a protest arose with the specific desire to reduce national taxation in order to increase investment within the region itself.

Growing identity and self-esteem on the one hand, and the need for more local resources to reduce the social gap on the other, brought together several actors who became the leaders of the demand for absolute autonomy from the Spanish central government. In a short time, the city that wanted to be Athens, the capital of a peaceful planet, set out again on a new struggle, a new challenge that was anything but peaceful. The city that had set an example for its progressivism, and had made its football club a model the world over, began to see that peace as a basis for development was a myth, and began to rely on a contrast between local and national identity as a new engine for growth.

A disconnect between strategies, implementation, and perception also began to manifest. Barcelona went from being a sunny place where everyone could speak out to a symbol of an ideology that was possibly not even shared by a majority of the citizens. The assertion of global liberalism strongly influenced local perceptions. The Forum was thus a planning victory but a political defeat: A few organizations highlighted its weaknesses rather than its qualities, and the city began to gain a perception of the Forum as being made up of shadow rather than light.

The fourth and fifth strategic plans: Barcelona as capital of the Mediterranean macroregion

Barcelona's fourth strategic plan, drawn up between 2003 and 2006, placed the concepts of innovation, creativity, and knowledge at the center of its development vision. It sought the most appropriate ways to ensure the city's management would serve citizens, enterprises, organizations, institutions, and municipalities in the metropolitan area. Hand in hand with these strategies, powerful new urban transformations were planned. This urban planning was not the end point, but only the framework behind the idea of a city that was made up of flesh and blood subjects, all with their own passions and actions.

The fifth metropolitan strategic plan (Barcelona Vision 2020), presented on 2 November 2010, was the result of the joint work of more than 650 experts in different fields, who collaborated for more than a year to compose and shape a projection for the future in which Barcelona was proposed as the capital of the Mediterranean macroregion. The planned governance model indicated a progressive alignment between the metropolitan area's policies and those of the Catalan (regional) and Spanish (national) governments. Six challenges were identified, to be supported by activating five levers of change. These challenges were 1) sustainability and climate change through energy efficiency and pollution reduction; 2) international positioning (Barcelona as capital of the Mediterranean macroarea); 3) assuming the role of world leader in selected knowledge sectors (design, art, health, and sport); 4) competitiveness (promoting new economic sectors following the "Beyond 'bio' companies" approach); 5) attracting innovative talent; and 6) social cohesion (responding to the crisis by building a more balanced society through actions relating to education, culture, public space, social housing, and mobility).

The five levers of change referred to 1) a university and vocational training system capable of producing excellence, attracting talent, and fostering a closer relationship with the production and business sectors; 2) a business-friendly administration that was lean, efficient, and transparent; 3) a governance system capable of applying innovative ideas in the management of strategic projects for which coresponsible public–private leadership was required; 4) values of the future, to give new character to the city and its inhabitants; 5) and positioning in world markets (knowledge of foreign languages, an international airport, and a brand for the city).

The projects, organized by area of intervention, were subdivided into strategic and operational metropolitan projects in seven categories: 1) knowledge; 2) mobility and accessibility; 3) strategic promotion of economic sectors; 4) sustainability and the environment; 5) social and urban cohesion; 6) infrastructure and key facilities; and 7) international projection and talent attraction. A map indicated their distribution over the metropolitan area and the category they belonged to. The forty operational projects were grouped into different areas of intervention. For many, detailed analysis defined their allocated costs and financial resources.

The May 15 movement and a woman mayor

But a stronger reality was pressing at the door. On May 15, 2011, during the second Zapatero government, as a serious national economic situation developed as in the whole of Europe in the aftermath of the 2008 crisis, Spain witnessed and to a large extent also participated in the protests of the anti-austerity Indignados. A new political season was opening, in which bankers all over the world were being asked not to consider ordinary people as "puppets" in the hands of finance. The demonstrations resumed four months later, on October 15, when the protest went global. The young urban generation was rebelling against the very model that had excited their parents; and the parents were agreeing with their children, unlike in 1968.

Among the most intelligent and proactive opponents of what the city had created over time was the future mayor of Barcelona, Ada Colau, who was founder of the Plataforma de Afectados por la Hipoteca (the Platform for People Affected by Mortgages), the first group aimed at supporting people who were finding it difficult to pay their mortgages (the so-called IPAs), which had started a powerful campaign against evictions in November 2010. Colau became the movement's spokesperson in 2012, and in 2013 presented the Congress of Deputies with a petition containing more than 1.4 million signatures, demanding a bill for certain fundamental rights related to housing and debt repayment, including payments in kind. Two years later, she founded Guanyem Barcelona, an alternative party to the socialist model that had governed the city almost uninterruptedly from 1979 to 2011. At the head of a coalition called Barcelona en Comù, which also included the Greens, representatives of Podemos, and the United Left, on June 13, 2015 Colau became the first woman to be elected mayor of Barcelona (she was reelected, not without difficulty, for a second term in June 2019). But what is the new city model she is working on? Does it completely contradict the glorious past of Europe's most exemplary city?

Barcelona constitutes a true urban paradox: the paradox of a growth so strongly desired and sought at any cost that it becomes unbalanced, and is seemingly lost in the eyes of most of its citizens.

Future

The demand for autonomy, the need for social inclusion, pride in one's traditions, impatience with too many tourists... Is Barcelona the European city that corresponds to San Francisco? Is Catalonia the European California? A mythical place, the first destination of every young person who wants to travel, a place of leisure and entertainment without rules, a center of creativity and innovation, but also a social space where inequalities are becoming more and more evident and unbearable?

On June 18, 2020, the mayor Ada Colau was pictured with the president of the executive commission of the strategic plan, Jordi Martí, and with the coordinator of the association for the strategic plan, Oriol Estela, in front of the mayors of the thirty-six municipalities. The plan for the revitalization of the Barcelona metropolitan area was based on two new objectives: to overcome the crisis caused by the pandemic by focusing on "economic and social progress to reduce inequalities" and for the municipalities to work together to develop new projects against the climate emergency. The programmed agreement for 2030 (the Compromìs Metropolità 2030) envisages six main lines of action: 1) improving the health of citizens; 2) building a more sustainable food system at all levels, regarding both production and consumption; 3) promoting the reduction of pollution with respect to international treaties; 4) boosting reindustrialization, with a focus on Industry 4.0; 5) encouraging the integration of research and innovation with economic sectors and public policies; and 6) substantially increasing the amount of housing suitable for citizens in the metropolitan area.

The challenge is set, but it is not the same kind of challenge as in the past. The problem is not just Barcelona; rather, it is the global context. Cities now no longer have to compete with each other but have to cooperate, find common horizons, experiment with innovative social and environmental solutions. To survive in the short term, we must look even further ahead. Will we be able to give citizens the right lenses to do so?

However, this new challenge is not easy to face. It is a balanced challenge, one that should not take place only within the context of development, but should also address the containment of inequalities, and bring back into the public sphere certain major responsibilities that urban politics delegated too hastily to private investments, themselves tied to international finance. Indeed, although much appreciated for the substantial work accomplished over ten years, the coalition led by Ada Colau—who, by law, could not serve again as mayor after two terms—was defeated in 2023 by the Socialist candidate Jaume Collboni. In the final hours before the city council vote, he managed to reach an agreement with both the Popular Party and Colau's own Comuns, resulting in a sudden reversal at the expense of the coalition headed by the Catalan separatists led by Xavier Trias.

A very confused situation, emblematic of how Barcelona can still imagine itself as a European leader in sustainable development and social cohesion (so much so that national leader Pedro Sánchez decided to convene there a meeting with the mayors of Rome and Paris to envision a new European future starting from its cities), but which still has not found solutions for the path opened in 1988 with the first strategic plan. A path based on a healthy balance between innovation, industrial production, skills, attractiveness, with universities and cultural institutions playing a leading role in bringing to Barcelona thousands of new residents, both temporary and permanent. A path pursued with seriousness and awareness, and yet one that has also brought Barcelona close to default: political default, with the idea of becoming the capital of an autonomous state, Catalonia, separated from Spain and nearly in conflict with it (at least in the local imagination); and social default, with friction between citizens and tourists—a true urban paradox in the very city that had most strongly pursued a development model based not only on standard tourism, but also on experiential tourism on the one hand, and on events and congresses on the other. A model that has never been fully renounced but kept almost in the background, and which every day seems to be undermined by crowds of culture enthusiasts who disregard (at least partially, since they are largely given no alternative) the impact of their actions on the urban fabric.

Starting from Barcelona, the urban paradox has played out: the greatest openness (cultural, social, technological) has led to the greatest conflict instead of encounter. Citizens and tourists, institutions and investors seem poised against one another. The local crisis of the model born with the 1992 Olympics and celebrated around the globe for a generation now seems to have completely crumbled. But with what new vision can it be replaced—one that appears, and truly is, just as open and democratic?

2 Turin
From manufacturing to culture

A capital city in grey

Was it the march of 40,000 that declared the crisis at FIAT and in manufacturing, after the postwar economic boom, that was definitive? What is certain is that on October 14, 1980, the clash between blue overalls and white collars reached its peak, even though we really had no idea what was going on.

Up until a few months earlier, it really had been curfew time. The last stirrings of terrorism had brought fierce and visible clashes to Piazza Statuto, where today the Frecciarossa high-speed train arrives, connecting northeast Turin to northwest Milan in less than forty minutes. Extremist fringes gathered on Saturdays and Sundays, ready to clash, either an open clash of the right and left or the one disguised as the ultras of Juventus and Turin. We boys would stop playing ball on the cobblestones when we heard the squad cars (sturdy, aggressive green or blue Giuliettas, depending on the type of weapon involved) arrive at full speed to break up the opponents. But more than perceptions and personal memories (which it is our right and duty to keep alive, because we are forgetting all too soon not just what the Second World War was like, but perhaps even more what the 1970s were like in Italy and especially in the north), it is the numbers that speak.

Crisis

That city that in fifteen years had more than doubled from 600,000 to 1,375,000 inhabitants (an all-time high in 1973), in as many years lost almost 400,000 and returned below the 1 million it had reached on a highly symbolic date, 1961, the year of the centenary celebrations of the unification of Italy.

At the beginning of the 1970s, the suburbs, which had sprung up very quickly to house the more than 343,000 direct employees of FIAT (there were still many in 1961 who had been directly employed by Vittorio Valletta, president of FIAT from 1946 to 1966), were no longer the lively places to which communities from Basilicata and Calabria, from Campania and Sicily, from Molise and Veneto had moved, but areas of great hardship where loneliness prevailed, where drug dealing and Mafia control dominated, where unemployment and prostitution proliferated. These are the days recounted in films such as Gianni Serra's *La Ragazza di Via Millelire* (1980), the years that gave life to the myth of Turin as a grey, gloomy, unfriendly city, where there was no hope of improving one's condition (the hope that was at the root of the exceptional migration of the 1960s) and the certainty of decline prevailed.

Two books more than any others have recorded this historical moment: the very short and fundamental essay *Turin. A Sociological Profile* by Arnaldo Bagnasco,[1] and *Did You Know that Cities Can Also Die? Turin: A Documentary* by Carlo Cresto Dina and Franco Fornaris, an intelligent and successful attempt to construct a documentary made up of words and images taken from interviews with people who chose marginality as a place of action.[2] Between 1981 and 1993, the years of publication of these two volumes, there were a series of studies considering the actions on which the city's subsequent rebirth would be founded. In particular, the Fondazione Agnelli's research on the possibility that Turin could shift its focus from manufacturing to advanced technological innovation, anticipating certain global trends and rapidly becoming part of a new triangle, with Lyon and Geneva, based on scientific knowledge and the biomedical sector in particular—consciously abandoning its position as the third, fundamentally productive, part of the industrial triangle that also included Milan, the financial and commercial center, and Genoa, the logistics and energy hub.

---

[1] Arnaldo Bagnasco, *Torino. Un profilo sociologico* (Turin: G. Einaudi, 1986).

[2] Carlo Cresto Dina, Franco Fornaris, *Sapevate che le città possono anche morire? Torino: un documentario* (Turin: Pluriverso, 1993).

Relaunch

While at the university level, and even more so at the political level, efforts were being made to maintain the productive leadership and the centrality of the factory in the life of the Savoy capital, there were already those who saw the need to better balance the different sectors of the city's socioeconomic reality.

A first major renewal was the birth of the Book Fair in 1988. It was thought that such an initiative would give Italy a major publishing, literary, and cultural event on a par with those held in Germany, France, Great Britain, and Spain, as well as Brazil and Argentina. Turin launched itself into the venture thanks to the vision and courage of an entrepreneurial accountant of refined artistic and cultural tastes, Guido Accornero, who, seizing on the suggestion of Angelo Pezzana, a cultured and committed bookseller, involved the major Italian publishers in a gamble that had immediate and very surprising success. While the Lingotto was about to close its doors as a factory to be reimagined as a commercial trade fair mall, the pavilions designed by Nervi in the 1930s transformed Torino Esposizioni for five years from a symbolic place for the presentation of new cars at the Salone dell'Auto into a center of national cultural debate—in an Italy that was about to face one of the strongest and most unexpected sociopolitical changes in its history. Held in May to launch summer bestsellers, the first Book Fair had been inspired by two guardians of the local imagination, the journalist Giovanni Arpino and the writer Primo Levi, who both passed away at the end of 1987, just as Giovanni Agnelli was commissioning the great American painter Larry Rivers to paint a portrait of Levi, the chemist and author of *If This Is a Man*, and the anniversary of the first publication of *The Young Nun*, the novel with which Arpino had made his name with the general public twenty-eight years earlier, was being celebrated. For this reason, to remember Arpino and to affirm with pride the liveliness of Piedmontese culture, an anastatic copy of *The Young Nun* was given to all the 100,000 visitors who visited the pavilions of the Salon thanks to the Confesercenti business association.

It was an incredible burst of creativity that ran through Turin in May 1988: Guido Accornero not only brought all the major Italian publishers to the Salone, and had the Fair inaugurated with a memorable speech by Nobel Prize for Literature winner Joseph Brodsky, but also invented youth volunteering and ordered authors such as Natalia Ginzburg, Claudio Magris, Jorge Amado, and dozens of others to tour the city, opening up courtyards and private homes, shoe shops and butcher shops for them. In this he was certainly inspired by the popular muse of Carol Rama, one of the greatest Italian artists of the last century and one of Accornero's close friends.

Barely five years had passed since the Zampini scandal, which in 1983 had shaken Turin's political structure, undermined the reputation of the communists led by Diego Novelli (mayor of the city from 1975 to 1985), and provoked a series of self-criticisms in the local system that would anticipate—once again, Turin was the forerunner—the imminent national *mani pulite*, or the nationwide judicial investigation into political corruption of the 1990s. In this climate of potential renaissance, the city was preparing to inaugurate the controversial Continassa stadium for the World Cup that was scheduled to be held in Italy in 1990, and had yet to find a way out of the national imaginary that perceived it a cold and reserved city, far (not just physically) from everything and everyone.

The 1990s and the direct election of the mayor

The World Cup passed quickly. Italy exited very early, disappointing the fans who had staked everything on Brazil stationed precisely in Turin, mythologized for the *torcida* made up of beautiful girls in costumes that accompanied it, but defeated by a cynical Argentina.

Developing the stadium was controversial. It was part of a broader plan to modernize the nation's sport and recreation provision, but it was linked to the unorthodox administrative practices that were rampant, especially in Milan, during the construction of the third metro line. The crisis in the national government coalition between the Christian Democrats and Socialists, which had been able to control both domestic politics and relations with major international interests in the 1980s, also affected Turin, which had been governed for some time by the Socialists first and then by a secular coalition, headed by Valerio Zanone's Liberals, who were among the first to relaunch research and leisure as potential new urban assets. But the time was not ripe for this, and a complete review of urban governance had to wait until the storm of *mani pulite* had passed. The scandals that followed one another in Italy between 1991 and 1992 led to a veritable civil revolution, the most long-lasting outcome of which was the end of the parties of the First Republic and the exercise of rather more direct democracy, especially in urban areas. It was decided that the election of a mayor should no longer take place according to name agreements made by the parties that won the elections but, in the English manner, by directly electing the first citizen, the head of a coalition that explicitly campaigned for election.

A coalition against decline

In Turin, the long-time mayor, Diego Novelli, was challenged. Novelli was the champion of a communist administration that aimed at improving conditions in the community and keeping dialogue open between FIAT, its workers, and the rest of the city; he was spokesman for the idea of a factory city, a production hyperdistrict, that had been born in the 1950s and was destined to influence the imagination of Italy's first capital city for decades.

Novelli's challenger was Valentino Castellani, a political outsider, a Catholic, professor at the Turin Polytechnic, and president of the Consorzio Informatico, which was creating the new telecommunications infrastructure required by a city that was about to enter the 21st century. Castellani led a new coalition, the Alleanza per Torino (Alliance for Turin). This was influenced by the ideas of Enrico Salza, who promoted the interests of small and medium-sized enterprises gathered around the Turin Chamber of Commerce; he had also commissioned a study entitled *18 Ideas Against Decline*, which highlighted the challenges that the city would face over the next few years. Surprisingly, a search for the new yet also for the reliable and trustworthy meant that Alleanza per Torino won the ballot and Valentino Castellani entered the Palazzo di Città as the new mayor. The challenge to imagine a new future for the city had begun.

Special Project suburbs

The coalition, especially the most important aldermen, included people who had worked with Novelli for a long time and knew the city very well—among them Eleonora Artesio and Fiorenzo Alfieri. Castellani, who had brought with him from the university and polytechnic a number of very experienced and capable professors (including, for example,

Giorgio Donna, a lecturer in business organization who was able in a short period to wipe out the budget deficit and get the city's financial investments back on track), asked Artesio to run the Peripheries Special Project, which framed the theme of urban space in a totally new way. Peripheries were not so much those places far from the city center, but rather those spaces that were perceived to be (and were) distant from decision-making. Places close to Palazzo di Città, the seat of the mayor and council, such as Porta Palazzo, the city's largest and liveliest market, were studied in detail. The inhabitants and, above all, the shopkeepers were involved in a process of listening and making collective choices, not only totally rethinking the services offered in the large square that had been home every day for over a hundred years to over 400 stalls selling food and nonfood products, but also debating relational cohesion before economic development plans were implemented, in the awareness that the latter proceeds from the former.

The first strategic plan

Turin's first strategic plan was born along the lines of that of Barcelona. Rereading them now, they seem to be two brothers born of the same father but with different mothers, one Spanish and one Italian. It was not like that, though, but rather a conscious and self-serving cloning. Having managed to balance the budget thanks to the meticulous work of Giorgio Donna, and having approved the master plan drawn up by Vittorio Gregotti and Augusto Cagnardi, based on discussions that dated back to the 1980s, at the end of August 1995, Castellani no longer wanted to hear talk of decline but of revitalization. To this end, reelected for a second term in 1997, he set up a Development Forum in which the city's economic and social forces would participate in an advisory capacity. Seeking to make Turin much less dependent on the industrial system linked to the automotive sector and its supply chains, and imagining a future based on balanced sectors such as trade, tourism, and higher education, following the examples of Lyon and Barcelona, discussions began on what methodology to adopt.

The proposal to follow the Catalan model came from Fiorenzo Alfieri, former councilor for education in many Turin city councils, who was well acquainted with Barcelona's councilor for tourism and sport, Enric Truno, honored by the IOC for his role in the 1992 Summer Olympics. In a disruptive interview during the summer of 1998, Alfieri said that creating a new promotion plan for Italy's first capital city was essential. Castellani seized on this suggestion, and the idea was born to directly invite the mayor of Barcelona and his councilor to transfer to Turin the method they had applied to follow up the exceptional impact of the Olympics. Pasqual Maragall, Barcelona's charismatic socialist mayor until 1997, became the president of the Scientific Committee of Torino Internazionale, first a project and then an executive association. Alongside him were figures such as the communications genius Milton Glaser, the inventor of the I♥NY logo, as well as scholars who were dedicated to analyzing Turin society such as Arnaldo Bagnasco. These major international figures and other experts began to work together with Castellani's councilors and eminent representatives of civil society, those who had already come together to write the *18 Ideas*. Among them were figures such as Enrico Salza, the president of the Chamber of Commerce; Rodolfo Zich, the rector of the Polytechnic; Anna Martina, head of communications of the Gruppo Finanziario Tessile (the most important fashion group in the area); Elda Tessore, president of the tourist development agency and former superintendent of the Teatro Regio; and Andrea Pininfarina, the industrialist who was the heir to a tradition of world-famous automobile design—all ready to devote themselves freely to their city.

Much the same was happening in another great Western metropolis, Pittsburgh, which was emerging from under the shadow of its previously dominant steelworks to enter the 21st century with a new look and feel. An entirely private entity, Pittsburgh First, had been set up to achieve this. In Turin, however, the model was one of collaboration between public and private sectors, with a mayor who assumed responsibility for change without taking charge. Castellani was adept at taking a step back from the work of the commissioners who had worked on the strategic plan, and he avoided taking this to the city council to be approved by councilors who were inattentive and perhaps even incapable of understanding what was going on. Thanks to Barcelona's example, the project was clear and well organized: There were nine working groups (later reduced to six), a secretariat of mediators, a top-level chairperson for each group, and an operational coordinator. A year's work and more than 2000 participants in some eighty meetings, most of them involving small groups, eventually produced a strategic vision with six lines of action, twenty objectives, and eighty-five actions. One of these was the candidature of Turin as the venue for the Winter Olympics (discussed in the next section).

It is important to emphasize that the strategic plan was based on an in-depth analysis of Turin's position in 1997.[3] The study was a major work of coordination, not an original production but a collation of all the research that had been carried out by experts, both local and nonlocal. The only new addition was a survey on perceptions of the city, conducted by Censis and coordinated by the director of that institute, Giuseppe Roma, based on over 4000 interviewees, about 2000 Italians and 2000 foreigners. Based on the data, and including working groups and a totally voluntary advisory board, considerable detail was provided regarding the actions to be undertaken, as well as the operational responsibilities, costs, and timeframe. The document was signed on February 29, 2000, and the significance of this was such that a parallel agreement between FIAT and the trade unions was signed the same morning, to help it come to fruition.

The vision envisaged a new role for Turin on the European chessboard. After forty years of an industrial monoculture, which had at one time seen more than 230,000 FIAT employees, the strategic plan envisaged a city that was decidedly more balanced and, above all, in which there was a new role for education and culture, and a decisive acceleration in the presence of women and young people in the labor market.

Infrastructure, governance, education, entrepreneurship, leisure, environment and social cohesion were the six major areas shared by all participants. The pact between the sixty participants who had signed the plan envisaged the immediate creation of an association whose tasks were to monitor the actions for which ownership, funds, and timeframes were clear; to directly promote projects that did not have clear ownership or sufficient autonomous funds; and to promote the plan to the media, investors, opinion leaders, and national and European institutions. This led to major strategic initiatives, such as Torino Wireless and Torino Automotive, Torino World Design Capital, and the Salone dei Mestieri. Local and regional politicians took note of the examples of Barcelona and Pittsburgh, Bilbao, Glasgow, Munich, and Stockholm, among others,

---

[3] Torino Internazionale, *Piano strategico per la promozione della Città* (Turin: December 1998), can be found online: see https://www.torinostrategica.it/wp-content/uploads/2013/03/I_dati_fondamentali.pdf.

and ascertained best practices and opportunities for Italy, and specifically Turin, from their experiences.

The Olympic bid, the system of intermediate bodies, and the reorganization of the municipality

Would the strategic plan have been so successful if Turin had not simultaneously won the opportunity to host the Twentieth Olympic and Paralympic Winter Games between February and March 2006? History does not allow us to rewind, but a statement made by Arnaldo Bagnasco at the time perhaps explains better than any other reflection the role of the Olympics in relation to the strategic plan. Bagnasco, who found himself obliged to get involved with the strategic plan immediately after the Olympics title was awarded on June 19, 1999 in Seoul, was able to comfortably transform one of the eighty-five actions envisaged by the assembled community into what he brilliantly described as "a powerful engine for the strategic plan": It was a kind of accelerator, a boost, an inescapable goal that strengthened the pact between the document's signatories.

A double act of courage had lined up two pearls of equal importance: a document with clear and important aims and an event to accompany its realization. Considerable discipline was required in order not to crash a timetable that was running two timeframes simultaneously: 2006 for the Olympics and 2010 for the plan. With hindsight, it could be said that the Olympics came too soon, that it would have been better to have a ten-year plan for everything, to spread the changes, to give greater quality to some of the planned urban transformations, and greater depth to the social and economic transformation. But the history of cities cannot be set in stone: One should plan for the best, but always have the flexibility to seize opportunities when they arise and make the most of them.

There were those who tried to undermine very complicated governance. While on the surface everyone seemed to agree, a struggle for absolute power soon broke out between those in Palazzo Civico and those leading the Olympic Foundation. Their interests were convergent but also potentially conflicting. Credit must be given to Sergio Chiamparino, Castellani's successor, who did not want to listen to the sirens advising him to take the whole pot that was on the table, consisting of urban transformation and sporting event together. Chiamparino, who had coordinated Castellani's candidacy, was nominated as mayoral candidate following the sudden death of Domenico Carpanini, deputy mayor during Castellani's second term, who died of a heart attack during the first electoral debate against Roberto Rosso, who was later defeated by Chiamparino. A skillful mediator, an enthusiastic economic researcher, a great hiker in the mountains, and a lover of card games and bowls, Chiamparino did not appreciate either the strategic plan or the Olympic events—so much so that once the 2006 experience was over, he did not enthusiastically support either a second plan, to give operational continuity to the first, or an event such as Italia 150, which was supposed to complete, through specific urban transformation projects, the transition of Turin from a 20th-century city to a 21st-century city. But we will return to this shortly.

The Turin of 2001, the city that the then fifty-three-year-old Piedmontese politician found himself leading almost by fate, was made up of many intermediate bodies, created to accelerate the transformation from a one-company town. These were not only the association for the strategic plan, which was actually incubated by two hybrid entities, Investimenti a Torino e in Piemonte (ITP) and Turismo Torino (the public–private consortium for the promotion and tourist reception of the city and its metropolitan area), but also the Turin Convention Bureau and the Turin Film Commission. The presidents and directors of these bodies were leading figures such as Andrea Pininfarina, Marco Boglione, Josep Ejarque, and Gabriella Ghigi. Turin recruited the best to make the city's project of change a reality. To attract talent, there is no other way but to set a good example—and to make systems less bureaucratic.

In Turin at the time, the strategy was clear—for the city to be perceived as Italian in all the aspects loved by foreigners and Italians alike: warmth and color, culture and cuisine, style (in design, fashion, cinema), the grace and sincerity of welcome; and also for the city to become European in its objectives. Therefore, in addition to the numerous intermediate bodies born in the shadow of Castellani's first and second terms of office—and not so loved by Chiamparino, who little by little, first as mayor and then as regional president, reduced their influence and autonomy—the city also enacted many internal reforms. A general director with very broad powers was appointed—and for this role the nationally renowned manager Cesare Vaciago, already at the highest levels in the Italian Post Office and Railways, was chosen. This was the most significant local development based on the municipalities: While in Turin, Vaciago redesigned the city's entire internal organization, making it super-efficient. In Milan in 1997, the newly elected mayor Gabriele Albertini called on Stefano Parisi, former head of the Department of Economic Affairs of the Prime Minister's Office and of the Department of Publishing and Information, to assume the same position.

Focusing on culture: heritage and animation

Turin has focused on culture and tourism, making the Spanish model implemented simultaneously by Barcelona and Bilbao its own. The aim has been to overturn the perception, revealed by a 1998 Censis study, that the identity of the Piedmontese capital was perceived (correctly) as hinging on three closely related names: FIAT, Agnelli, and Juventus.

The first great symbol of Turin's changing landscape was a monument par excellence: the Mole Antonelliana. Designed by the architectural engineering genius Alessandro Antonelli, born in Ghemme in 1798 (the same year as Leopardi) and a pupil first of the Brera Academy in Milan and then of the Albertina Academy in Turin, the Mole was built over a very long period starting in 1863; it was completed in 1897, ten years after the death of its designer. Conceived as a Jewish temple, it then housed the Museum of the Risorgimento, a function it performed from 1908 to 1938, when the new museum was opened in Palazzo Carignano. Over time, however, the Mole has remained something of a monument to the Jewish community, who in the years of its construction had been forced to sell the building to the City of Turin, bartering it for an area in the San Salvario district where the city's current synagogue stands. Mayor Castellani found a new purpose for this incredible architectural work, which from 1889 to 1908 had been the tallest masonry building in the world. In 1995, on the one hundredth anniversary of the invention of cinema, the "seventh art," the dream of Maria Adriana Prolo, who for decades had collected memorabilia related to early cinema, began to take shape when the City of Turin decided to assign the Mole as the home of a National Cinema Museum, setting its inauguration for the year 2000.

The design was entrusted to the French stage designer François Confino, who had already designed interiors for the Centre Pompidou in Paris, the Natural History Museum in Los Angeles, and the traveling exhibition Cités-Cinés in the years 1987–1990. On July 19, 2000, the new museum was opened, and immediately its direction was entrusted to Alberto Barbera, one of the greatest connoisseurs of world cinema and former director of the Festival Cinema Giovani—which was later transformed into the Turin Film Festival.

The almost simultaneous birth of the Turin Film Commission in September 2000, conceived as part of the city's strategic plan at the suggestion of Marco Boglione, founder and managing director of BasicNet, the company that owns the Robe di Kappa, Jesus, K-Way, and Sebago brands, among others, made the city's objective clear: to become a center of production, promotion, and attraction around the theme of cinema as an art form that strongly represented the 20th century, in which Turin had been a leading protagonist.

Discussions and actions also relaunched two other of the city's fundamental cultural assets: the Egyptian Museum and the Reggia di Venaria Reale (Palace of Venaria). The former, by virtue of the collections acquired by the House of Savoy in agreement with the French cultural world at the end of the 19th century, has always housed the second largest collection of Egyptian antiquities in the world, the first being, of course, in Cairo; the latter was in reality a ruin without a purpose, and the dreams of two politicians, Piero Fassino and Valter Veltroni, rapidly transformed it, thanks to a shrewd and rapid use of European resources and private resources from the region, into a leading tourist destination.

These two projects were strongly accelerated under Turin's first strategic plan. It was discussed whether the Egyptian Museum should be moved from its historical location, shared with the Academy of Sciences and the Sabauda Gallery, to the new urban center of the former Savigliano Workshops; but it was decided to keep the original location, so as not to deprive the historical center of an important attraction. Resuming that debate became worthwhile in the years that followed, when the lack of cultural relevance of the suburbs, which were increasingly becoming dormitory districts, crowded into the local and national debate. Barcelona would have had no concerns about moving a museum from the historic center to a new center, making culture into an engine of social cohesion. Today, perhaps the discussion would lead to different conclusions, but twenty years ago, moving the museum, even in a very innovative Turin, was impossible.

The redevelopment of the Egyptian Museum was made possible by new governance with a decidedly innovative model; this made it the site of an unprecedented public–private partnership in which for the first time a state asset was linked with private financiers (in this case the Compagnia di San Paolo Foundation, the majority shareholder of Intesa Sanpaolo, Italy's leading bank). Managers were put in charge of both the museum's presidency and its management, but great care was taken to ensure that the director was also a great expert in the field. Work began in the early 2000s, and the museum was ready to be inaugurated in time for the Twentieth Winter Olympics, in the winter of 2005–2006.

The Reggia di Venaria Reale was a third pivotal element in this policy. Not just historical Turin but the entire metropolitan area was to be transformed and a new, powerful cultural district was to arise from the symbolic place of Europe's most important automobile district. The Savoy royal palaces consist first and foremost of the Castello di Rivoli (since 1984 the site of the first museum of contemporary art in Italy, thanks to an extraordinary collection of *arte povera*[4] in comparison with which the second floor of London's Tate Modern pales into insignificance, and capable of attracting millions of visitors on its own), the Palazzina di caccia di Stupinigi, and the Castello di Moncalieri. These sites, along with others, have been UNESCO World Heritage Sites since 1997; but of all of them, the one that seemed to have the least potential was the Reggia di Venaria Reale itself, an unfinished project (like Rivoli in part), which had attempted to challenge the beauty of Versailles.

The Reggia di Venaria Reale is rightly considered one of the greatest restored European sites, but also one of the most important recent cultural and tourism planning successes in Italy and indeed the world. After its nomination as a UNESCO World Heritage Site, the redevelopment works began in 1998, with a total expenditure of 280 million euro; this was financed thanks to national funds from the Gioco del Lotto (the national lottery) and European funds. Less than ten years later, one year after the Turin Olympics, the palace was inaugurated, immediately becoming an essential tourist destination, with an average of 1 million visitors per year.

---

[4] *Arte povera* (literally "poor art") is an avant-garde art movement that emerged in Italy during the late 1960s. The term was coined by Italian art critic Germano Celant in 1967 to describe a group of artists who were challenging conventional art practices and materials. By embracing unconventional and deliberately humble materials, these artists sought to disrupt traditional notions of art and its association with wealth, grandeur, and the commercial art market.

These are only the three most significant elements of Turin's cultural renaissance campaign. The city was also illuminated by the *Luci d'artista* (artist's lights) invented by Fiorenzo Alfieri in 1998, while in the ten years between 1998 and 2007, its most important squares and streets (Piazza Castello, Piazza San Carlo and large portions of Piazza Vittorio) were pedestrianized, bringing to fruition a dream visualized in the late 1980s by Giuseppe Dondona of a city in which cars no longer dominated public space, an important role was assigned to underground car parks, and there was sustainable mobility, including the first underground line, a railway link, and the new Turin Porta Susa station.

Lyon's model for urban spaces and Barcelona's model for attracting events and innovation were used to the full, allowing Turin to experience a unique, perhaps unrepeatable season, in which public works succeeded in compensating for the difficulties experienced by the great private industry that had dominated the urban scene for the previous forty years.

Stabilization

The year 2008, as in many other parts of the world, was also a terrible one for Turin's urban economy. Just when the city seemed to have emerged from its role as a one-company town and to have found a different balance, based on the four pillars of knowledge, enterprise, leisure, and social inclusion, represented not only by the new cultural infrastructures that have already been mentioned, but also by the doubling in size of the polytechnic, the redevelopment of Porta Palazzo (Europe's largest open-air market), and the birth of trade fairs such as Mestieri in Mostra, the city suffered a double setback.

The first of these occurred a few weeks before 2007 came to an end: It was one of the worst work-related accidents in recent Italian history. On the night of December 6 and 7, inside one of the largest steel mills in Europe, the former Teksid that had become the property of Thyssenkrupp, a fire caused by an irregularity in the operation of a production line killed seven workers and injured one very seriously.

Turin's working-class rightly demanded that more attention should be paid to what was happening. The mayor, Sergio Chiamparino, who was very shaken by the affair, decided to suspend any kind of event that might disrespect the victims. Among other things, the inauguration of the Turin World Design Capital was canceled, an event that, after the 2006 Olympics, the 2007 Winter Universiade, the launch of the new Cinquecento in the summer of 2007, and the opening of the Reggia di Venaria Reale, aimed to consolidate Turin's role as a leader in urban innovation and in the integration of the industrial past and the future of a city of innovation, culture, and design.

The second setback came at the beginning of August. While riding his Vespa to work on a midsummer's day, Andrea Pininfarina, symbol of the new Turin in which doing business and creating beauty found their synthesis in the word "design," was involved in a dramatic car accident, and lost his life. Andrea was not just an entrepreneur; he was capable of holding together very different visions, and above all had a truly unique national and international network. As president of ITP, Andrea had been behind the candidature of the Piedmontese capital as the first World Design Capital. It was also he who had explained the importance of "industrializing" the events: of choosing a theme for the city each year, of making these themes the subject of a methodical and rigorous programming that would bring together the need for the visibility of manufacturing sectors with an urban life that was able to attract businesses, talent, and tourists as a single, consistent chain.

It was time to stabilize the successes achieved through the investment in Olympic design and to relaunch them with new ideas, whether in wireless, design, or a new automotive model, which had just found its champion in Sergio Marchionne. Having steered FIAT through its most serious crisis since 1899, 120 years later Marchionne crowned the Agnellis' dream: He succeeded in buying Chrysler (so pivotal that this was announced by Barack Obama). Turin seemed not to be giving up in the face of world crisis and was relaunching itself once again—not only on the production line, but also on the cultural front.

The planning of the 150th anniversary of the unification of Italy had been underway for two years (after Turin had lost to Milan as the Italian candidate city for the 2015 Expo). Turin, the first capital of the kingdom, had been a strong protagonist of the centenary celebrations that had been held in 1961; these had featured Walt Disney (who brought the first Circle-Vision 360, forerunner of the IMAX, to Turin), the writer and film director Mario Soldati, and Andrea Pininfarina's grandfather, Battista "Pinin" Farina, who had designed the industrial pavilion. For 2011, the city wanted to conclude the renewal process started in 1993, continued with the activities planned between 1998 and 2000, and implemented steadily thereafter until 2007. The Italia 150 project (named after Italia '61) was to make the city a new center from a macroregional as well as an international perspective. If the objective of the first strategic plan, entitled Torino Internazionale, was to put Turin back on the map of both production and consumption, the new plan, which was worked on between 2007 and 2008, envisaged a "city of knowledge" at the service of the rest of Piedmont, much of Lombardy, and Liguria. Just as Turin 2006 had been the central focus for the first strategic plan, it should have been for Italia 150.

But perhaps the success of the first plan had loosened governance; the lack of external enemies had—as is so often the case—begun to sow envy and a desire for strong autonomy even among those who were promoting change. Turin was no longer one team, but many small teams competing. Chiamparino, who had been able to keep the tiller steady in 2001, directed a progressive dismantling of the intermediate structures during his second term in office, gradually recentralizing. In addition, he had dismissed the idea that headline events could replace all or part of the productive city, which instead had to make a comeback; the focus had to be more on a new welfare model than on an increased ability to generate turnover in sectors other than the traditional ones.

Future

On March 17, 2011, President of the Republic Giorgio Napolitano inaugurated the official celebrations for the 150th anniversary of the unification of Italy at the Teatro Regio in Turin. However, Turin did not represent all of Italy; rather, it was only the most willing, most motivated, most prepared to present events as a coherent system of activities. Indeed, it was in 2007 that Vice-Premier Rutelli, the brilliant coordinator of the 2000 Jubilee, had decided that, unlike in 1911 and 1961, Italy would not be celebrated in a single city (in 1911 it had been Rome with Turin to a limited extent, in 1961 it had been Turin and others to a very limited extent, since in 1960 Rome had also had the Olympics). The redistribution of resources to infrastructural activities that had little to do with the jubilee of the nation allowed works in progress such as the Perugia airport or the new theater of the Maggio Fiorentino to be completed. However, this did not distract the media from the focus on Turin, the only city to have a coherent program of exhibitions held in a symbolic place: the Officine Grandi Riparazioni (OGR).

The OGR was the space that best expressed the city's future potential. Earmarked in the first strategic plan as a new large center for contemporary art, at the service of both the Castello di Rivoli and the Galleria d'Arte Moderna, it had already been involved in the selection and promotion of *Luci d'artista* (artist's lights), and boasted successes such as the installations on Monte dei Cappuccini curated by Rebecca Horn and the Fibonacci series illuminating one of the four sections of the Mole. The OGR had also already hosted the 2008 World Congress of Architects and Biografia di una città, the large exhibition on the transformation of the urban center curated by Carlo Olmo. In 2011, it was the turn of the historical exhibition *Fare gli Italiani* (Making Italians), which was curated by two of the most prominent Italian historians, Walter Barberis and Giovanni De Luna, and set up by the talented designers of Studio Azzurro, as well as *Stazione Futuro* (Future Station), a view of Italy in 2061, curated by Riccardo Luna with the advice of Joseph Grima.

The OGR was in the center of the new Turin: a large, covered square between the Politecnico, near the Intesa Sanpaolo skyscraper designed by Renzo Piano and the Porta Susa high-speed train station. As in a novel, the future history of the city should and could begin here. Instead, somehow, this was where it ended. "To complete" is perhaps a verb that does not suit Italians, and perhaps even less so the Turinese. What should have been the setting for the city's greatest celebration, in which the capital of national culture was returned to this place after 150 years, became a playground for political and economic clashes. Instead of opening up to younger generations, making space, the city folded into a successful diarchy, that of the "two Sergios" (Marchionne and Chiamparino), obscuring a host of small and medium-sized projects with a centralist vision of the factory and the common institution.

Thus, when in 2011, celebrating an anniversary in which he had believed, with a certain skepticism, Sergio Chiamparino left Palazzo Civico, the forty-year-old Michele Coppola, who was capable of expressing the many talents that had emerged during ten unforgettable years, was not appointed mayor. Rather, it was a politician of long standing, one of the longest-lived and most capable "professional politicians" of the Left in the 1980s and 1990s: Piero Fassino. Undecided until the very end whether or not to take part in the electoral competition, Fassino (former secretary of the Democrats of the Left from 2001 to 2007 and before that minister of Foreign Trade and Minister of Justice, who entered politics as a nineteen-year-old in 1968, a passionate expert on foreign policy who was appointed European Union envoy to Burma in 2007), is one of the most prominent figures to have become mayor of Turin. But, like Valerio Zanone, who became mayor of Turin in 1990, Fassino failed to make an impact on the city, despite his great experience and tireless work.

The Castellani effect, his promotion, together with many of his councilors, of all the city's economic and cultural components, including before the strategic plan a Forum for Development, was not taken up by Chiamparino who—as briefly mentioned earlier—preferred a less open view of local development, and brought the focus of public actions back within the municipal system. Fassino, owing to his real politically minded attitude, did not renew either the language or the content of the Turin project—even though he was much appreciated by the citizens. His five years as mayor were devoted more to sorting out the finances that the 2008 crisis and unsupervised investment management had decisively battered, making Turin (eighteen years after the redevelopment during the first Castellani legislature) one of the most indebted metropolitan cities in Italy. Fassino made great efforts as mayor to bring about new international alliances, particularly with France, which could prove very important in the following decade; but the national economic situation linked with local conditions did not allow him to implement some of the major projects that had been initiated in the strategic planning at the beginning of the millennium. It could be said that he was the right man at the wrong time: He continued his efforts in the cultural sector, of which he was a great advocate, and brought to the city a series of new ideas and contacts, but both the tools and the resources available did not allow him to plan a further relaunch of a city that desperately needed a new vision and different representation. These were the years in which two strongly contrasting movements emerged on a national level: the rise of Matteo Renzi as the undisputed and almost monocratic leader of the Democratic Party, and that of the Five Star Movement at a national level. Turin was the thermometer—as has often been the case—of this tension, and while Fassino sided with Renzi in several battles born out of the renewal of the ruling class, intolerance for a top-down model of development management began to grow in the city. The local debate focused on the concept of the "Turin System": what was conceived in the early 1990s as a necessity, teaming up and putting all the local actors around the same table, began to be perceived as arrogance of the elites, who were unable (paradoxically) to renew themselves precisely when they themselves were calling for renewal.

What is happening internationally, with an ever more evident clash between the economy of finance and the real economy, is now weighing heavily on the city; Unfinished socioeconomic diversification and incomplete governance (I am referring here to the metropolitan area, which had fascinated experts as well as business interests since the beginning of the millennium) keep too large a segment of the population out of the development game—and, above all, out of its narrative. Two very significant trends have emerged from the vote analysis: The center-left entrenched in the city center (inhabited by the upper-middle class) is chosen by those over fifty-five years of age, while the young and those living in the so-called peripheries, which are at the center of the electoral challenge, vote for Five Star. Chiara Appendino (mayor of Turin from 2016 to 2021) presented herself as everyone's leftist; but her legislature, born to give a strong impact of change, almost immediately clashed with structural elements and there were internal quarrels within the party that supported her. The vision it proposed was one of strong opposition to the last twenty years of local history.

No to the TAV (high-speed trains), no to big events, no to an attention to the quality of life, no to the expansion of cycle paths, no to a stop to cars—or at least this is how the legislature was perceived. But the momentum of the electoral victory, based on the votes of young entrepreneurs and professionals added to that of the "people of the suburbs," rapidly lost its momentum, owing to two exogenous and one endogenous factor. The first of these was the decline of the Five Star–Lega coalition, which governed the whole of Italy for a short period as a completely abnormal combination that was born out of an interest in exalting the values of each party and not in finding a new collective identity for the nation. Second, the lack of safety at Piazza San Carlo, where one person died and more than 1500 were injured in a stampede during the UEFA Champions League final match between Juventus and Real Madrid in 2017 (in urban histories, football and sports in general often return as accelerative factors, often positive but just as frequently negative), brought the mayor and part of her entourage to court. Finally, internal management governing the relations between councilors and management, and between management and municipal offices, brought about a great contrast between announced projects and their actual impact.

We are now nearing the end of Stefano Lo Russo's first term, which brought the city back under Democratic control after five years in the hands of an administration composed exclusively of representatives of the Five Star Movement, founded in October by Beppe Grillo and Gianroberto Casaleggio. The Five Stars, who governed Turin from 2016 to 2021, could have used the Savoy city as a major testing ground, and at the beginning something of the sort did take place—although driven by a desire to be "different" from everything that had happened in Turin between 1998 and 2011, with a style of presumption and vindictiveness that was hardly acceptable. The Five Star ideology, shaped by Casaleggio along the lines of a kind of Olivetti-style communal socialism, could have been an interesting fit with the field of technological innovation in which Turin was moving at the time, as it searched for a new national role in light of the now irreversible European crisis of local mechanical manufacturing and the need to focus on a new leadership class of young people and, above all, new entrepreneurs. This was something already foreshadowed between 2007 and 2008, which the title of World Design Capital, as mentioned above, could have accelerated, but which was in some ways slowed by the arrival and vision of Sergio Marchionne at the helm of the FIAT group, compounded by the still heavily industrialist outlook of a mayor like Sergio Chiamparino.

But the actual management of Chiara Appendino's five years as mayor ultimately failed to make a real impact on Turin's society—at least judging from the subsequent election results. The 2022 elections, held still in the post-pandemic climate, saw the center-left prevail with 60 percent of the vote in the runoff between Stefano Lo Russo, backed by a coalition composed of the Democratic Party and five allied groups, and his center-right opponent Paolo Damilano, a well-known entrepreneur also active in numerous cultural initiatives in the region (formerly president first of the Cinema Museum and later of the Film Commission).

From the outset, the Five Star Movement trailed far behind in the polls and then in the final outcome, with the former mayor under investigation for the events of Piazza San Carlo (the tragic night of June 3, 2017, when three people were killed and 1,672 injured after panic broke out during the remote viewing of the Champions League final between Real Madrid and Juventus, held in Cardiff). This made it impossible for her to defend her record, as she could not run for a second term.

The project with which Stefano Lo Russo won in October 2022 placed at its core the idea of building a city tailored to university students—rich in cultural and social opportunities—while paying close attention to bridging the traditional interests of the productive classes with the most advanced forms of social innovation. The latter found expression, in parallel to an unfruitful administrative phase, through the work of several highly capable figures who identified high-quality pathways. Among them: Torino Social Impact, led by Mario Calderini, professor at the Politecnico di Milano and former coordinator of the Alta Scuola Politecnica Torino-Milano project; Davide Canavesio, entrepreneur and former president of both Environment Park and Torino Nuova Economia, the joint company tasked with developing new projects on part of FIAT's historic Mirafiori production site; Matteo Robiglio's social housing projects, developed within the new company Homers in collaboration with Mario Montalcini; and the continuous visioning work of Luca Ballarini, which gave rise to projects such as *Torino Stratosferica* and *Torino Open House*, as well as the annual event *Utopian Hours*, Italy's first festival dedicated to "city making."

All this testifies to the city's extraordinary vitality, still powerful in the artistic and musical scene that had made it "the place to be" between the late 1990s and early 2000s. A leadership that the Five Stars, despite their criticism of the model of Turin as an Olympic city, not only failed to oppose but ultimately reinforced: indeed, 2021 will be remembered less for the elections than for a hugely successful special edition of the Turin International Book Fair—founded in 1988 and relaunched by the talent of Silvio Viale and Nicola La Gioia—as well as for the city's first edition of the ATP Finals, which arrived in Turin thanks to the very same Appendino administration that had once rejected and repudiated major events as drivers of urban development.

Once again, however, Turin seems to be starting from there: in 2022 it hosted the first edition of the new International Festival of Economics, while also trying to leverage two new manufacturing assets—aerospace and biotechnology—in order to give legs and breath to companies that had been tied for too long to the traditional automotive sector. And in 2025 it once again hosted the World University Games, invented by Primo Nebiolo (reviving a tradition begun in 1923) with the first postwar edition held precisely in Turin in 1959.

Building on the most advanced reflection on how to shape the future to 2030—coordinated by Filippo Barbera and colleagues, under the title *Turin 2030. Future-Proof*; the result of interviews, webinars, data surveys, and potential assessments based on the SDGs, the Sustainable Development Goals—the city that was once the first capital of the Kingdom of Italy identifies six "missions": industrial reconversion; the metro-mountain vision; enabling social infrastructures; shared spaces; environmental and intergenerational justice; and cultural and artistic production. A valuable piece of work, not sufficiently read or studied by the local elites, who at present seem not to have rediscovered the thread of a discourse made clear by the first strategic plan: a medium-to-large city (as in the European context, in this case) must know how to specialize and continually find new vocations without leaving anyone behind, while at the same time remaining conscious of its role as a regional capital.

The Lo Russo administration, in its first term—which will end in May 2027—has certainly been able to take advantage of the investment opportunities offered by the debt-funded National Recovery and Resilience Plan, Italy's program for managing EU *Next Generation EU* funds approved by member states to foster economic recovery after COVID-19.

There are seven areas of action: the city of proximity; the multicentric and mobile city; the city of innovation and development; the city of networks and social impact; the city of opportunity; the international and interconnected city; and the metropolitan city. In all, more than 300 projects are planned by 2026, with over €717 million in NRRP funds, another €81 million from React funds, and €149 million from Pon Metro Plus funds.

Twenty years after the Olympics, Turin has received another massive injection of resources—but this time without a crucial ingredient: enthusiasm. Mayor Lo Russo, endowed with strong political skill, great pragmatism, and undeniable knowledge of the administrative machinery, has yet to win over his fellow citizens, who see no new horizons ahead. Above all, Turin is losing young people, especially the most talented ones. A study by the "Giorgio Rota" Center, conducted by Luca Davico, shows that while the city manages to attract a substantial number of new university students every year, it ultimately ends up with a negative balance. Unlike Wroclaw—whose case we will examine later—Turin still fails to position itself as a hub where knowledge, skills, and entrepreneurial spirit intersect. On the contrary, many companies, after the third or fourth generation, end up selling to larger international operators, effectively placing their staff and development markets in the hands of foreign funds.

Both of these potentially negative trends are highly visible, and measures to counteract them are already underway: in the 2025–2026 academic year, public transport will be free for university students, while Stellantis (the umbrella brand encompassing Fiat—with Alfa Romeo, Ferrari, Lancia, and Maserati—and PSA—with Citroën and Opel—after Marchionne's masterstroke of bringing Chrysler, including Jeep and Dodge, under Turin's control) is reassessing the city's central role in research and development.

Another player that could bring major benefits to the Piedmontese capital is NewCleo, Europe's first group dedicated to developing policies on next-generation nuclear energy. Yet the wider population is not actively engaged in this vision of the future and remains entangled in less strategic but no less urgent issues—chief among them the perception (contradicted by the data but constantly amplified and dramatized by the media and political parties) that immigration takes away jobs and causes a marked rise in petty crime. This national dynamic has in Turin produced new forms of intellectual segregation, with clashes among the "new poor" particularly visible in the Barriera di Milano neighborhood, where most immigrants of Maghrebi origin are concentrated.

As recent, well-documented studies such as Hein de Haas's (just published in Italy by Einaudi) make clear, migration is a standard feature of human life on the planet, and no real growth trends can be identified. And yet populist narratives continue to feed on such claims and permeate urban life.

Turin is responding—as it did at the beginning of Mayor Castellani's first term in 1993, with a significant and prophetic cultural initiative promoted by his culture councillor Ugo Perone under the title *Identity and Difference*—through a series of very concrete measures, in particular by investing about €25 million in the Aurora and Barriera districts, areas that have struggled the most to achieve integration between southern Italian migrants who came to work at Fiat in the 1960s and 1970s and the Maghrebi, Albanian, and Romanian migrants who arrived between the late 1980s and the end of the 20th century.

However, these very concrete actions—such as those concerning the restoration of the rivers (in addition to the Po, the Dora and also the Sangone are of great importance), inspired by the extraordinary results achieved in other European cities such as Lyon, which will be discussed in a later chapter—have not yet provided new overall momentum, not only for the capital but for the entire metropolitan area.

Unlike the period between 1999 and 2006, Turin—by then fully and legitimately a tourist city, a valued destination, and regarded, especially in the rest of Italy (once rich in prejudice), as a beautiful and livable place—has not yet managed (to use a metaphor dear to one of its most important analysts, Arnaldo Bagnasco) to "clear the rocks." The economic transformation from a metalworking city to one with a diversified, asset-based economy remains incomplete. These are also months in which close attention is paid to the new economic policies of the newly elected U.S. president, Donald Trump, whose tariffs could deliver a significant blow to the regional economy, strongly characterized by food and beverage and, in particular, the wine and confectionery sectors.

The coming decade appears decisive for Turin: it must decide whether to align itself more closely with its metropolitan area, explicitly linking its new master plan—which Mayor Lo Russo will try to have approved before the end of his first term and on which he will build his candidacy for a second—with a "metro-mountain" dimension strongly demanded by both local territories and experts (above all, the authors of the report coordinated by Filippo Barbera mentioned earlier). Moreover, Turin no longer seems to be innovating in certain sectors that never became truly strategic, despite declarations to the contrary: first and foremost medicine, which in the past earned the city no fewer than three Nobel Prizes (Salvador Luria in 1969, Renato Dulbecco in 1975, Rita Levi Montalcini in 1986) but now sees the "City of Health" project bogged down in architectural and financial disputes, without following an exemplary model such as that of Pittsburgh, which will soon be discussed in detail. A second and final point concerns culture: with NRRP funds, a new major public library will be opened in the former Turin Exhibition Center, designed by the talents of Pier Luigi Nervi and, it seems, Ettore Sottsass, and repurposed for library use by the Isola studio, which had already demonstrated skill and courage in restoring the Egyptian Museum to its best form. Yet the centrality of reading as a fundamental element of local culture—not only supported by the International Book Fair, founded in

1988 by Guido Accornero, but also by the network of publishing houses that includes such names as Bollati Boringhieri, Einaudi, Loescher, and Paravia (still active, though for the most part now owned by groups based outside Turin)—does not yet appear to be becoming, as in the case of Wroclaw cited earlier and analyzed later in this volume, a true backbone of development.

Turin indeed has many arrows in its quiver, but it still seems to work too vertically, failing to build a genuine system—neither between public and private, nor among public bodies, nor among private actors. It has succeeded in making people forget the gray city it once was, where clashes between owners and workers became emblematic and turned into political conflict, intertwined with the dangerous events of the 1970s that made it a base for national terrorist movements such as *Prima Linea* and the *Red Brigades*. Yet its great effort to reinvent itself as a luminous city with *Luci d'Artista* is now being called into question (in a debate that also strongly involves its twin and eternal rival, Milan) in the name of a supposed greater concreteness and a demand to focus more on cohesion than on glitter.

The urban paradox has struck again: having escaped the industrial monoculture that had crushed 1930s Turin—the city of cinema, radio, chemistry, fashion, and soon after, television—the city now finds little satisfaction in its many new hypotheses of economic and cultural development, and wonders where it should place its bets. For a city with such a deeply military DNA, perhaps this was to be expected. But it was thought to have matured enough antibodies to give itself a more consciously and deliberately international dimension, one rooted in the multiple world's fairs it hosted between 1884 and 1902 and reaffirmed by events such as the centenary of Italian unification, the Winter Olympics, and much more.

Now what is needed is a new leap forward—one of quality as well as quantity.

3 Pittsburgh
Steel and disease

A demographic swing

Do you remember the first scene of *Flashdance*, the film directed by Adrian Lyne (who also directed *9½ Weeks* and *Indecent Proposal*), which in 1983, thanks to its screenplay and Giorgio Moroder's powerful music, won three Oscars? It is dawn. The protagonist, Alex, gets on her bike, rides down from the poor and hilly suburbs where she lives, crosses some of the city's more than 400 bridges, enters a factory, puts on a helmet complete with protective visor, and works until sunset delicately handling steel and aluminum. The dominant color is orange, the same as the rising sun and the warm lights along the Appalachian Mountains in the evening, but above all orange is the glow of the hot materials that the young worker must master. The city featured in these first four minutes is famous for its distant past of arms production, for its long excellence in steel manufacture, for the spectacular decline that has united it with Detroit and Cleveland, but also for its present of incredible recovery, around the hospital and the university, both born of the industrial patronage of the Carnegie family, who also endowed Carnegie Hall in New York—among much else.

Pittsburgh is one of the phenomena of the last thirty years: It had 300,000 inhabitants at the beginning of the 20th century, 650,000 in the 1950s, again 300,000 at the beginning of the new millennium. This demographic swing suggested disaster—the classic story of the shrinking cities of the golden age of great manufacturing, which must accept a far from golden decline and ask themselves what they did wrong; why all the wealth they created in decades of frenzied growth is not able to give more lasting roots to the community.

Unlike Detroit and Cleveland, however, Pittsburgh has not accepted its fate. Thanks to two mayors, Tom Murphy, elected three times between 1993 and 2005, and Bill Peduto, a baby-boomer who belongs to the lineage of the new Democratic mayors who grew up in the shadow of Obama's administration, the city has been able to transform itself and give itself a new destiny, treasuring those assets that the second half of the 20th century had forged and that the industrial and financial crises between 1979 and 2008 failed to destroy.

As Murphy himself, a politician who practiced his job as mayor by conceiving of his role as that of a manager in the service of the community, reminds us, cities that succeed must build their success on three basic elements:

- They must be well administered and safe, offer excellent educational opportunities, and have reasonable taxation.
- They must devote great effort to innovation in the economic sphere, seek out availability of capital, and wholeheartedly embrace entrepreneurial partnerships in which the relationship between public, private, and institutions is very productive.
- They must be fantastic places to live, offering a great quality of life, affordable housing choices, and a clear and shared vision of regional development.

These three fixed points of urban development philosophy are set out by Murphy in a text published at the beginning of 2011 for the Urban Land Institute,[1] to which the former mayor is now a consultant. They are dictated by an awareness of what has happened in the United States in the previous twenty years, with a relocation of production that has destroyed the working class, its rhythms, and its rules, causing millions of jobs to be lost, mostly replaced by what has been produced by the technological revolution, creating totally new professions, in the fields of health, education, and technology itself.

---

[1] Tom Murphy, *Building on Innovation: The Significance of Anchor Institutions in a New Era of City Building* (Washington: Urban Land Institute, 2011).

Crisis

It was in 1901 when J.P. Morgan (the great banker who transformed the financial sector and became the pacemaker of American industry) worked to merge the Carnegie Steel Company and many other steel factories into US Steel, which produced between half and a third of the national demand depending on the year. Pittsburgh turned the corner demographically, becoming the eighth most populous American city and attracting thousands of immigrants from all over the world, especially from Eastern Europe. From Pittsburgh came the steel to build the masterpieces of the American 20th century, from New York's Empire State Building to San Francisco's Golden Gate Bridge.

Pittsburgh's population reached half a million before the Second World War, driving further growth that was fueled by the war effort. Those were dramatic years, in which the factories stayed open twenty-four hours a day in order to produce 95 million tons of steel, which helped to defeat the German–Italian–Japanese alliance—which for its part fed on the Ruhr's industrial capacity and the ability of two other world-renowned entrepreneurial families, the Thyssens and the Krupps, who in 1926, following the American model, created the Vereinigte Stahlwerke (United Steelworks). Such industries produced, along with steel, two serious side effects: damage to the environment and to the people. Workers could do no more than work in temperatures that were difficult to bear and in air that was constantly fouled by gases and fine dust. Different types of illnesses emerged; hence the need for doctors and hospitals to specialize in the treatment of upper limb injuries, painful and deep burns, and bronchial diseases.

A little more than a century ago, between 1919 and 1920, just after the end of World War One, the first major trade union demands took place to reduce working hours, which were twelve hours a day, six days a week.

Just over a century earlier, an agricultural community had been established at the confluence of three rivers,[2] to serve the construction of the railway lines that stretched westwards over the Allegheny slopes. In the 20th century, these rivers lost their crystal clarity and became sumps into which industrial waste drained unchecked.

---

[2] Near Pittsburgh, the Allegheny and the Monongahela converge to form the Ohio River.

After World War Two, although the railway infrastructure and much of the urban development had reached their peak in the 1930s and 1940s, the economic boom nevertheless kept steel production alive for another twenty years, which paradoxically entered a crisis in the very year of its peak production, 1977. The collapse of the steel industry in the 1980s caused a deep economic depression throughout the Great Lakes area: Between 1979 and 1987, 133,000 jobs were lost in the region and unemployment rose by 15 percent. Steel production had now found new locations: India, China, Brazil. The blows of international competition could have been the end for Andrew Carnegie's town. For more than a hundred years, Pittsburgh had produced half of America's steel; its factories had churned out industrial products and weapons used in every conflict since the Civil War of 1861. Now all that remained of what had been referred to as "hell without a lid" was the world's worst urban pollution.

Relaunch

How did the steel city turn into a world center for health care, university education and research, and high technology in such a relatively short time? Why did the same thing not happen in Detroit, Bilbao, Turin? Can this experience be a model for Taranto, and also for Trieste? And also for some large Indian cities that will soon have to reflect on their own destiny, when the average age of the population reaches forty-five?

In reality, Pittsburgh was not only renowned for steel, but also the production of glass and precious materials and electronics components; it was a logistical center both for the transport of heavy materials and for the handling of large quantities of food; it was also involved in oil, given its proximity to Cleveland, and in cars, given the presence of the mighty Detroit. For much of the 20th century, Pittsburgh was third behind New York and Chicago as the headquarters of large corporations and had the largest share of ownership per capita. Centuries of wealth at their disposal and an open and combative ruling class, whose emblem—as Cruyff's Barca was for Barcelona—was the Pittsburgh Steelers, always owned by the Rooney family and led by local genius Bill Cowher, who took them to the playoffs for six seasons in a row in the 1990s, reviving the glories of the 1970s, when the Steelers had won four Super Bowls in six years.

From "steel city" to "tech town": truth or just a narrative? In the case of

Pittsburgh, as we will see further in the next section, it is indeed correct to speak of "resilience." The term, which for some years has dominated urban debate, harks back to what Jared Diamond conclusively explained in his masterpiece *Guns, Germs and Steel: The Fates of Human Societies*, a title that seems tailor-made for Pittsburgh.[3] Only a society that knows how to lose, only a community that has been defeated has the antibodies to succeed again. The Turin that lost FIAT put together all its talents, concocted a strategic plan, and organized the best Winter Olympics ever; then, back on top, it lost it all again because its ruling class no longer had any external enemies; it fought against itself and like Cronus ate its own children. In Pittsburgh, however, one of its sons, the aforementioned Tom Murphy, was elected mayor in 1993. His father worked in a steel mill, he had studied urban development, and he had all the talents to be a "can opener" for the community, someone who slowly opens a can of tomatoes and uses it to restore color and flavor to the city he lives in. The cans metaphor may remind us that Andy Warhol was born and educated in Pittsburgh. He never denied his origins and his hometown has dedicated an excellent museum to him in the cultural district that has replaced thousands of square meters of factories in a triangle of land between the three rivers. That museum, designed in 1989 and opened as early as 1994, was a first glimpse of the future for the mayor who had just taken office.

Pittsburgh really makes us think about what we might call a self-consistent urban economy. The three priorities framed by Murphy were achieved by systematizing what had been happening in some areas since the 1980s.

The hospital was the centerpiece of an influential redevelopment that took place in two tranches (the first in 1980 and the second in 1986, with a total value of more than $1.5 billion), which was accompanied by a total redefinition of role and perspective, with new management and new researchers specializing in transplantation (including one of the pioneers of this type of surgery, Thomas Starzl). It was home to some of the world's most advanced transplants, and also promoted important cutting-edge research into operations conducted on very young patients and into the use of advanced robotics.

---

[3] Jared Diamond, *Guns, Germs and Steel: The Fates of Human Societies* (New York: W.W. Norton, 2008).

At the same time, the University of Pittsburgh, one of the great educational institutions born in the late 19th century that made possible what Olivier Zunz, explaining its birth and growth, called, "the American century,"[4] was totally rethought and reorganized.

Thanks to the funds set aside by Andrew Carnegie and his heirs, Pittsburgh was not only able to cure the diseases that had afflicted three generations of citizens, but also to create excellence in various realms that gradually become international. In advance of other major Western conurbations, it was able to transform productive skills into "curative" skills. The focus of society is no longer on the quantity of the goods produced, but on the quality of life of citizens, starting with the health care sector, which is being joined little by little (even to the point of anticipating it in everyday life) by the cultural sector, whether classical art forms, live entertainment, or digital content production.

Now for nearly two decades, after a crisis that lasted as long, Pittsburgh is rated as one of the most livable cities in the United States and the world. Who would believe, especially seeing it from Italy, with our distant and distorted perception, that the Steel City would be named among the best cities in which to live by *The Economist* in 2005, 2009, and 2011, usually ranking between twenty-fifth and thirtieth globally? In 2010, *Forbes* recommended Pittsburgh as a place to raise a family, and in 2007 as the seventh cleanest in the world! What "livability" means is quickly stated: less crime, a lower cost of living, and cultural opportunities. This could, in short, be considered an extraordinary model for many European cities.

It was no coincidence that Obama chose Pittsburgh as the venue for the 2009 G20: The city was an ideal example of the change the president desired for large manufacturing areas. The summit was held inside the David L. Lawrence Convention Center, which Mayor Murphy conceived to host large international medical conventions and which later became one of the symbols of the city's rebirth, with a public investment of about \$1 billion; this, combined with more than \$3 billion in private investment, also enabled the construction of a new baseball stadium and the Heinz History Center, more than 25,000 square meters of exhibition space dedicated to Pennsylvania's past, present, and future.

---

[4] Olivier Zunz, *Why the American Century?* (Chicago: University of Chicago Press, 1998).

The Convention Center was, at the time of its use as a venue for the G20, the largest building in the world certified as totally green. Murphy understood that in addition to medical science and culture (in a city that for nearly a century had had a very low education rate and a mortality rate that was far higher than the national average), there was a need to invest with great care and to accelerate the issue of sustainability. By the end of his third term as mayor, the great wave of crisis that had hit the city and caused the loss of more than 40 percent of its population seemed to be over. Pittsburgh had gone from being a "steel city" to a "tech town," and Pittsburghers, the residents of the city but also of the metropolitan area (a region of about 2.5 million people) were proud to be "eds & meds based," This was founded on excellent education for all and on attracting talent—but also on creating so much of it locally that it could be "distributed" to the rest of the country and around the world; while the medical sector ensured good health for all residents and was a model for the entire United States.

Stabilization

Having exhausted the experience of a son of the "old steel city" as mayor, it was now up to a representative of the "new tech town" to lead the city along the path to stability that had started in the early 1990s. Pittsburgh did not hesitate to support one of the youngest mayors in US history, Luke Ravenstahl, who at only twenty-six was ready to lead the city to new heights. A career in politics was his family destiny: His father was a powerful magistrate and his grandfather had been a Pennsylvania state representative in the nation's 1976 bicentennial.

Ravenstahl was not immediately elected mayor, but took over from Bob O'Connor, who had won the election after Murphy but had become seriously ill with a rare brain tumor. As much as O'Connor (himself a steel mill worker for some time) represented the common people, Ravenstahl was a symbol of a new elite focused on further improving the quality of the city on three fronts: reducing the impact of taxes on citizens; increasing opportunities for college entrance for those who were finishing high school; and fostering access to politics and public roles for representatives of traditionally disadvantaged sectors (women, young people of color, LGBT activists). The elections that confirmed him as mayor after O'Connor's sudden passing were held in 2007, and Ravenstahl won them unopposed; in fact, Bill Peduto, who would succeed him in 2015, withdrew before the final ballot.

Ravenstahl reinforced some of Murphy's policies and O'Connor's early insights, reinforcing the concept of active citizenship service for the city under the banner of "ServePGH," which was launched in September 2009, a few weeks before the G20. It focused on five main actions:

- "Love Your Block"—seeking resources to revitalize the city "house to house."
- "Redd Up Zone"—recruiting volunteers to keep the city clean at all times.
- "Snow Angels"—recruiting temporary volunteers to help those with problems during the colder months.
- "Mentors' Initiative"—devoting free time to help younger people choose a job.
- "Civic Leaders Academy"—building better civic skills for local leaders so they would be better prepared to meet the urban challenges of the future.

Despite many proposals, and some major urban planning operations such as the revitalization of Market Square—the large central area that in the 1970s was decaying owing to traffic and crime, and between 2009 and 2010 was completely pedestrianized and transformed into a new commercial and tourist attraction—Mayor Ravenstahl was perceived as acting quickly but much less sincere than his predecessors. Not surprisingly, there were many disputes with both the local community and law enforcement during his terms in office. Ravenstahl represents the new challenges for mayors of US and world cities in the new millennium: It is not enough to work to foster and complete the transition from manufacturing to services; rather, it must be done with a maximum of transparency and a minimum of self-interest.

Future

Being mayor is increasingly a mission, and less and less a job.

This was the case for Bill Peduto, the city's mayor until January 3, 2022, who had always served his fellow citizens, to whom he offered a new vision for the future in 2016, two years after his election, after serving as a city councilor since 2002. Thanks to his long experience of listening to the city council, Peduto understood that there was more than just growth, redevelopment, wealth, and skills to talk about; the stress that the city of Pittsburgh had had to endure to get away from the stereotype of "global city/steel town" had not brought all citizens to the same level of competence or, more importantly, allowed them to understand the changes that had taken place. Now, thanks to a worldwide project launched by the Rockefeller Foundation in 2015, entitled "100 Resilient Cities," Pittsburgh built an ad hoc pathway: "1 Pittsburgh / 4 P."[5]

The "four Ps" with which the city has responded to the challenges of the 21st century are People, Place, Planet, Performance. It is these "four Ps" that address the decisive question of the local without being localist, as French philosopher Bernard Stiegler put it—one of the basic questions for urban development in the last two decades.

Pittsburgh's response is a true manifesto of collective commitment, more than a strategic plan. It is born not only out of concrete goals (as if the city were a business to be run well, as in Murphy's time), but also out of value pillars that go beyond Ravenstahl's "aesthetic" vision, making it an "ethical" issue: The city is to be a place of collective, balanced, and coherent growth.

Let us read the four points carefully:

> PEOPLE
> Pittsburgh will empower ALL residents so that they can prosper and grow the individual communities that make up the city, ensuring that everyone achieves. WE will be an inclusive city that values diversity well; all residents will have equal access to the resources and opportunities the city has to offer.
>
> PLACE
> Pittsburgh will use its land to give equal benefit to all residents; to increase social cohesion, connectivity, public health, and ecosystem health; and will do so while protecting the city from natural and exceptional hazards, present and future. WE will design our infrastructure with present and future needs in mind in its form and mainte-

[5] See http://www.p4pittsburgh.org/.

nance, providing benefits and services to all neighborhoods in times of tranquility as well as in times of crisis.

PLANET
Pittsburgh will achieve long-term environmental quality by making use of wise stewardship of available resources, with great intent to reduce our ecological footprint.

PERFORMANCE
Pittsburgh will work closely with those living near our territories and our private partners to optimize land-use planning and related decision-making.

The resilience strategy adopted by Pittsburgh thus integrates an economic vision not with the theme of consensus but with that of accountability; with a conscious ability to hold together interests of individual groups with the broader interests of the urban community. To this end, the experts called upon to structure the actions that would help to achieve the set goals not surprisingly stressed four functions that I would like to call organizational (and which I would not want to be listed as political): convening working groups based on local leadership; establishing a structure for governance and progressive institutionalization of the pathway; establishing measurement values for the planned actions; and integrating the physical resilience of urban spaces with civic engagement activities and public events. For the sake of clarity, the methodology even provides a timeline for implementation: There is an initial phase of initial project sharing, internal coordination related to the different proposals that have emerged, time for fundraising, and then a final phase of project acceleration, leading quickly to implementation.

Peduto and his advisors realized that in the transformation game there are many who are left behind.

There was no malice here, no deliberateness. The changes were so difficult and all-consuming that keeping the city alive and building a new image and new development models was no small feat; neighboring Detroit and Cleveland could not do it. But, to quote again from the dossier with which Pittsburgh applied for funds and expertise from the Rockefeller Foundation, even though the city achieved a very high ranking as far as "livability" was concerned in the 1910s, wage disparities and the issue of "housing segregation" are still not resolved to this day. With a population that is 65 percent white and 25 percent black, with 10 percent of other communities present, Pittsburgh ranks seventeenth among the fifty US metropolitan areas for the largest share of black population. And the disparity in income, for a family of four, is indeed significant: $37,000 is the average for whites, $21,000 for black and Hispanic-speaking citizens. All this is coupled with a strong aging demographic, greater than in other metropolitan areas.

This is an interesting set of data for Italian cities such as Taranto or Turin, and for other European cities such as Bilbao and Manchester. Cities that with a sudden shock and with many and large investments overcame for some time the trauma of having lost the leading role they were assured in the 20th century by ubiquitous manufacturing at the urban level, and yet were unable to fully make up for the loss of wealth and skills that that city model had offered to their many immigrants.

It is no coincidence that the Pittsburgh model has been evoked in Italy to give new hope to communities such as Taranto, which have a reservoir of truly unique historical and natural beauty, but unfortunately lack the "strategic resilience" that for some thirty consecutive years the residents living at the confluence of the Allegheny and the Monongahela have been able to demonstrate.

Two actions included in the Pittsburgh work plan, titled OnePGH, were very interesting: finding jobs for those who needed them most through a public–private agreement with major recruitment players, and the explicit goal of bringing 20,000 new citizens, especially young people, to the city to cope not just with its declining population but especially with its aging population. The launch of the whole operation coincided with the bicentennial of Pittsburgh's birth as a city—the moment from when it had legislative autonomy with democratically elected representatives. This choice was also symbolic of the change of pace from the "programmatic oligarchy" that for twenty years had directed a city that had always voted for the Democrats, to a strong broadening of the decision-making base, based on just a few ideological elements but primarily activated by numerous projects on the ground.

Peduto, and with him other new mayors who were appointed during the Obama presidency (such as Bill De Blasio in New York and Ed Murray in Seattle, two cities in their own ways symbolic of innovative growth models and also seeking not to leave behind a significant portion of their populations), have looked to Washington not as the decision-making center of power, which they ask for the resources to implement necessary changes, but as the space in which they present new policy models so they can take on a national dimension. This has taken place while the contrast between the growth and revitalization of urban areas on the one hand and the disappointment of the rural periphery on the other has been becoming central to political discussions in the United States and elsewhere (we will touch on this issue both for Wrocław in Poland and also in Russia as well as in Turkey, key states in world geopolitics).

Peduto was able to launch this new phase of the city's revitalization thanks to some important data: the 17 percent growth in the population of young people between the ages of eighteen and twenty-four in the five-year period 2006–2010 (an obvious effect of policies to strengthen the university sector). and even its positioning as the third largest city in the United States in terms of the percentage of highly educated population in the group born between 1985 and 1995. The city's gaze has thus shifted to the millennials and their ability to be a ruling class in a contradictory demographic context—with more and more white seniors demanding new entitlements and a population of young people who are more globalized but also for that reason less rooted, and therefore less willing to bet everything forever on one place. To retain these young people and allow them to build families who want to stay in Pittsburgh, after the city has somehow allowed them to be part of a system of growth that is sufficient for innovation, technology, and services, the city must be energy efficient and enhance not only cultural but also natural assets. These are two efforts that are very much present in the resilience strategies proposed in 2016 and approved (and financially backed) by the Rockefeller Foundation; they are particularly relevant to the policies that concern the redevelopment of green areas and riversides that are no longer energy engines for the manufacturing sector but rather accessible spaces to be enjoyed by every segment of the population.

If Pittsburgh can redistribute the wealth that is produced through an urban model based on education and care, it can truly become a symbol of a new, more equable urban segment, in which there will be no poorer neighborhoods and richer neighborhoods, but a continuous exchange of functions and values in which the reciprocity of relationships will be the backbone of the community. This functional egalitarian model will be capable of holding ideas and utility together. This postsocialist challenge was not coincidentally born in a city most of whose elderly still belong to labor associations that have fought hard battles for the quality of place and way of working. In this model, affection for one's fellow human beings overrides private interests. In addition to Warhol, Pittsburgh was also the birthplace of one of the great American novelists of the last fifty years, David Leavitt: He is gay, as Warhol was, and they both have fought logics of inequality with a talent and passion for their intellectual work that has been truly exemplary. Unlike Warhol, who combined artistic talent with business talent to the point of making himself the banner of a generation that can make its talent profitable, Leavitt looks at cities as spaces in which stories of families navigate a necessary and difficult balance between individual experience and collective responsibility. It is perhaps in his novels, and even more so in his short stories, that we can find the model for this new urban society, a meek society, through which we can focus on the future.

A future that today looks above all to the role of the Black community, which in 2022 elected with 70 percent of the vote yet another Democratic mayor—once again someone who rose from the grassroots, having entered politics at 18, right out of high school.

Ed Gainey, born in 1970, is the first African American chosen by his community as mayor, and for the past three years he has been successfully advancing the work of his predecessors, with a particular focus on the safety of his fellow citizens. In 2021, violent crime and homicides had risen by 46 percent, and residents—especially in the poorest neighborhoods—demanded strong control by the local police. Thanks to a special intervention program called REACH, gun violence among minors was brought down to zero in a very short time.

Beyond public safety, in his first thousand days in office Gainey has significantly expanded the ability of Pittsburgh residents to own a home or to live in high-quality social housing at affordable prices—a deliberate policy to make Pittsburgh truly a city for everyone. At the same time, all chronically homeless people have been registered and offered the chance to live in community spaces where they can feel not only less isolated and less vulnerable, but above all welcomed and understood—an initiative combining regulatory, medical, and especially psychological expertise.

Climate has also received special attention, not in vague terms but with a precise understanding that climate change disproportionately affects the poorest, who generally live in less protected and less regulated areas. For this reason, Gainey has emphasized neighborhoods at risk of severe flooding, which in the near future could wipe out entire families. Other measures include completing streets that unnecessarily divide neighborhoods, thereby reducing deep social separation.

The next step is to give a voice in city council committees to those who normally do not participate or are not heard—either because of their "diversity" or their lack of trust in institutions. At the heart of Gainey's new vision for Pittsburgh is a genuine "civic education for all," transforming ordinary recreational spaces into hubs of lifelong learning, with special attention to ensuring universal access to sports while also providing everyone with specific STEM skills.

The Pittsburgh of 2050 must—and can—be a community of nearly two million people, only 15 percent of them living in the historic city proper, with all others easily connected and accustomed to extremely low energy costs thanks to effective use of wind-based systems. A city in which the most vulnerable are guaranteed a minimum income, permanent access to healthcare, and a first-rate basic education.

4 Lyon
The government of light

The perfect city

> France has screwed us over! Yes, fooled! We gave ourselves to her like a woman in love. Here with us there is not a single influential man who has not studied in Paris: France, always France! Even among ourselves we speak in French. We know your literature better than you do.

This anecdote is related by George Simenon, and it concerns the relationship Romanians had with the French in the 1930s; but it could—*mutatis mutandis*—be perfectly used for the relationship Lyon has with other European cities, especially with some Italian cities such as Turin and Milan.

Lyon is a perfect city. At least that is how it appears. So perfect that there is almost no need to talk about it. Yet nothing that has happened in the last fifty years is random. Nor is it linear. In a nation like France, where only Paris counts, establishing itself as an innovative urban area has been very difficult. But Lyon has done it. How?

Crisis

The turning point was the late 1980s. While socialist grandeur unfolded in the capital with some billion-franc projects, such as the Grande Arche de la Défense, the Très Grande Bibliothèque, and the collective use of the Beaubourg was celebrated, Lyon was embarking on a course of international repositioning of extraordinary quality. Prior to that date, consistent with traditional long-term management by a single mayor, it had been Louis Pradel, a radical who later became the symbol of a civil society that was very much connected to widespread small-scale commerce, who held the office from 1957 for twenty years, dealing mainly with large new infrastructures, starting with the construction of the La Part Dieu business center, which, as Elisa Rosso recalls in a comparative study between Lyon and Turin compiled in the early 2000s,[1] he considered a tool for the internationalization of the city and its businesses and for general modernization. After Pradel and after Francisque Collomb, who governed Lyon from 1977 to 1989 and was confronted with the growth in demographic and political clout of neighboring Villeurbanne, led by socialist leader Charles Hernu, the new mayor—whose election coincided with the bicentennial celebrations of the Revolution—was Michel Noir.

But let's take a step back.

The Chamber of Commerce and Industry and a new articulation of public–private relations

The economic development and internationalization of Lyon has long been administered by the city's Chamber of Commerce and Industry (CCI). This interface function is allowed in France by an ambiguous legal statute that makes chambers of commerce public institutions, governed by a political executive elected from among the entrepreneurs, but subject to the direct tutelage of the Ministry of Economy and Finance.

In Lyon, which has a strong liberal tradition, the CCI was founded in 1702; it has been an important player in the city's economic development since the early 20th century. After being the main promoter of industrial zones, and manager of some public infrastructure, the CCI changed its role in the early 1970s, becoming a real economic development agent.

The CCI's metropolitan-scale economic development policy is based on the scheme for the Lyon–Saint-Étienne–Grenoble urban areas that was drawn up by the Organisation d'Etudes d'Aménagement de l'Aire

[1] Elisa Rosso, *Governance metropolitana a Torino e Lione. Analisi comparata dei processi decisionali in alcune politiche di trasformazione urbana*, PhD thesis in Social and Comparative Research, University of Turin, Department of Social Sciences, 2004. The first part of this chapter draws on this contribution in several places, courtesy of the author.

Métropolitaine (OREAM). The CCI operates over a wider area than that of the Communauté Urbaine de Lyon (the Urban Community, COURLY) and argues that the development of the Lyon agglomeration should be designed on a functional territory that goes beyond COURLY's administrative boundaries. Within the framework of the policy of balancing metropolises, the ICC supports the importance of the Part Dieu business center project and the construction of the Satolas airport to improve the city's international positioning. The integration of economic development policy with the body's activities is down to one person in particular: Jean Chemain, who remained at the CCI from 1971 to 1995, first as director of the Agence pour le Développement Economique de la Région Lyonnaise (ADERLY) and then of the CCI itself, profoundly influencing its structure and mission.

ADERLY was established within this framework in 1974, with the participation of both public institutions and local industrialists; organizationally, it is thus independent of the Délégation Interministérielle à l'Aménagement du Territoire et à l'Attractivité Régionale, and, although it is part of the institutional system, is a public–private partnership. Led by the ICC, which has developed dedicated expertise, since its creation ADERLY has decided to take as a reference for its activities a territory larger than COURLY, the functional area defined by the OREAM study, which straddles three *départements*. It is in this new territory, the Lyon Urban Region (RUL), that the Lyon agglomeration presents the greatest diversification of economic activities. ADERLY's tasks are to promote Lyon to the outside world, negotiate industrial conversion, and attract industrial establishments and research centers. For example, the project to relocate the science departments of the Ecole Normale Supérieure to Gerland is being overseen by this agency.

Between 1970 and 1990, in an underdeveloped area on the margins of COURLY's institutional activity, as were the policies of internationalization and economic development, the ICC became an institution of political experimentation, an incubator of new ideas, a place of elaboration and design of innovative strategies, partly because of its proximity to the economic and industrial world. Within the ADERLY, thanks to the personal relationships between its members and the expertise of officials deployed by the state, economic development issues that concerned private individuals, large industrial groups, and central government were institutionalized.

The importance of the CCI as a promoter of economic development has diminished with the decentralization laws that assigned more space to local communities. Real estate and land policy since 1982 and competence in the field of economic development since 1999 have been entrusted to urban communities, which have significantly greater financial resources, especially in comparison with the highly diversified activities of the CCI (training, economic development, management of public infrastructure). In the 1990s, KICs faced a major reduction in the fiscal resources available to them, and at the same time saw their centrality as public–private interface structures diminish. In Lyon, the transformation of the economic system and patronage mediation channels and the gradual growth of different needs of socialization between entrepreneurs in emerging sectors eventually reduced the CCI's authority in decision-making processes, and its autonomy.

A new generation of civil servants

While the ICC saw its role fading, COURLY's technical structure, by contrast, gained in importance; it was the actions of officials, rather than those of politicians, that reinforced the idea of intercommunality in technical management, as in major projects. From undertaking the management of services and urban planning, COURLY entered the economic development sector, despite not officially having this competence. A new elite of politicians and civil servants began to emerge who were on the margins of the local decision-making system, but who understood the importance of a different articulation of public–private relations and of action in support of local development that institutions could undertake.

In 1978, the Agence d'Urbanisme de la Communauté Urbaine had also come into being, operating in the service of local institutions, a pivot point around which a new generation of local policies and politicians had been building. Slowly COURLY's services were being reorganized: From administration came the development of technical skills for preparing decisions and building real community policy. Sensitive to the problems of spatial planning, this new generation of politicians began to involve themselves in an innovative form of local development and management of spatial problems at the metropolitan level. The goal was the implementation of a planning policy that brought strategic and priority-selection functions back to the local terrain, broadening the gaze to the entire agglomeration, and moving beyond the traditional view that was limited to seeking funding from the state.

In the second half of the 1980s, within the Agence d'Urbanisme, which had urban study and planning functions, debate began about the revision of the General Regulatory Plan that had been approved in 1978, and a series of consultations between civil servants and politicians on the future of the metropolis was initiated. Reflection on these policies had the effect of producing a network of civil servants with a metropolitan perspective, who were interested in the issues of urbanism and planning: They were a new local technocracy who had the same thoughts about urban planning and shared the goal of enhancing excellence. The new generation of local politicians, still on the margins of the institutional scene, could thus lean on a network of civil servants who were trained in wide-area planning and the identification of policies of excellence in their attempts to enhance local development and attractiveness of the whole metropolitan area.

Michel Noir and the birth of Grand Lyon

In March 1989, Michel Noir was elected mayor. Already a minister, and thus a powerful figure with a national image, Noir gave legs to the strategic planning project "Lyon 2010. Un projet d'agglomération pour une métropole européenne," which had been presented in 1988, the first step in a new urban policy that was experimental and innovative compared with those being prepared for other French metropolises.

The document contained preliminary studies for the revision of the 1978 Schéma Directeur d'Amenagement et d'Urbanisme, a revision that articulated the final goal—that COURLY and sixteen surrounding municipalities would form the Syndicat mixte d'Études et de Programmation de l'Agglomération Lyonnaise. Civil servants from the Agence d'Urbanisme, together with COURLY and ADERLY, worked on the drafting of the project. It was novel in two areas. First, an attempt was made to legitimize the urban planning document through social debate and to involve economic actors in the definition of the objectives. Second, the document had as a goal the need to align Lyon with other European noncapital cities, thus abandoning competition with Paris. The document indicated five priority areas for action:

- the strengthening of economic development, the restructuring of areas for economic activities, the construction of major transportation infrastructure, the strengthening of higher tertiary activities, and the development of university hubs;
- the extension and improvement of the urban transportation system and connection with regional and national transportation system;
- the development of residential activity and the rehabilitation of public housing districts;
- the development of international functions and the improvement of the city's image (tourism, culture, promotion); and
- the planning of an environmental policy and improvement of the quality of life.

From a spatial point of view, the document identified places that were highly significant for future development, strategic spaces of agglomeration, which would benefit from specific actions and investments. The provision of long-term strategic goals strengthened the ties between the different actors in the metropolitan area, especially between COURLY and the municipalities of the first row, which felt they were associated with an overall initiative. The project actually referred to an area that was larger than the agglomeration alone and was close to the RUL, a scale that gave Lyon the greatest diversification of activities, thus being considered more appropriate than COURLY for planning and development. To coordinate interests at a level that so far lacked institutional legitimacy, the Lyon Urban Region Association was created in 1989.

It was Noir who chose the name of Grand Lyon for COURLY, to which he wanted to give an international role, thanks to the development of major urban projects (such as the Cité internationale) and the growth of the metropolitan strategy initiated in previous years. Noir's aim was the development of an economic development project, and for his commitment to economic action he earned the appellation "maire entrepreneur." To achieve the goal of modernization and development, he changed the organizational form and internal functioning of the institutions he presided over, creating several administrative areas in the fields of his interest and placing them directly under his influence. Actions relevant to COURLY's economic development had until then been based on financial redistribution, using COURLY's competencies at the financial level. For Noir, though, it was necessary to plan and implement major choices and priorities at a higher level, involving the entire urban agglomeration and on a scale that was suitable for economic development and internationalization. He thus chose to anchor his politics at RUL level, and became president of the association itself, seeking to conquer territory by accumulating executive functions.

Noir's action constituted a break with the past. Failing to cooperate with the municipalities of the row caused hostile reactions from their mayors, but also from COURLY's administrative and economic partners. The mayor of Lyon's power grab was not accepted in a political system that had been historically marked by a polycentric regulatory model. Noir's ambitious strategy, as mayor of a major city and a national politician, was not shared by the "notables" of Lyon's traditional right, represented at the political level by the president of the General Council of the Département du Rhône, Michel Mercier. Moreover, Noir's victory in the elections changed the political balance within the agglomeration where traditionally the mayor of Lyon and the president of the General Council were of the same political color. Noir's initiatives at RUL level were thus progressively obstructed by local political leaders to the point of institutional gridlock. The RUL became a political arena rather than a consultative entity. The metropolitan ambitions of Lyon's mayor clashed with the cautious attitude of the state, the detachment of the Regional Council, and the utilitarian concerns of the General Councils of the three *départements* involved. For the latter, the RUL was useful not because it established a common political agenda or structured a metropolitan territory of public action, but rather because it was a forum where the problems of each other can find political support for seeking funding from the state and the region.

The goal of Lyon's mayor was to structure a new political institution that was capable of stimulating economic development over a wide territorial area, but this was not accepted favorably by private interests or the local production system, who actively participated in ADERLY. One of the levers used by ADERLY for attracting outside businesses was the competition between municipalities brought about by the institutional fragmentation of the area, particularly in the fiscal field. As a result, ADERLY did not regard the establishment of an institution governed by local politicians that was in charge of economic development across the whole region as beneficial. Noir's internationalization strategy remained anchored on infrastructure production and the promotion of industrial zones, the fields over which the mayor had most control.

A judicial scandal ended the political career of Michel Noir. He was succeeded in 1995 by Raymond Barre. ADERLY, the ICC, the General Council, and the Regional Council established an agreement to oppose the RUL and Barre, after a year of debate, agreed to reduce its role, making it into an association that was oriented towards sectoral issues, and was in essence just a place where local politicians could periodically consult each other.

Relaunch

The strength of Lyon's position in the French and European landscape can be traced at least in part to the existence of a city plan that has accompanied the 1995–2005 decade of public policy action. Several planning documents have presented priorities for the agglomeration's development over time. The aforementioned "Lyon 2010" of 1988 came first, and it was followed by the 1992 Schéma Directeur de l'Agglomération Lyonnaise, which identified the need to add Lyon to the South European arc of regional capital cities and a desire to attract valuable international functions.

Internationalization dictated by Raymond Barre

The internationalization of the city continued to be one of Lyon's priorities during Raymond Barre's term in office. Elected in 1995, Barre, a former prime minister and politician of national influence, changed COURLY's system of government, which he felt was too centralized and traditionally based on a balance of power between COURLY and other regional or local actors. The new mayor assigned some of Grand Lyon's vice-presidential positions, traditionally reserved for the majority right, to reform-minded socialist and communist mayors in the row (Villeurbanne, Vaulx-en-Velin, Bron, St. Priest), thereby increasing the power of the communes over COURLY. Barre inaugurated a new way of governing the city, oriented toward a search for consensus and pluralism. He brought together almost all political forces in a consensual form of governance, through the identification of priorities and the definition of a "mandate plan," which contained precise indications of the choices to be made and the resources to be allocated. The internationalization of the city, according to Barre, could only be achieved through a collective project that involved the city's various interest groups in a manner that was open and transparent to the citizenry and involved public consultation. COURLY was at the center of this planning and involvement dynamic, in which political experimentation based on pluralism and interinstitutional dialogue was inaugurated.

To realize this ambitious political project, Barre launched some innovative public policy processes and implemented a reform of COURLY's internal organization. He created an entity, the Mission Prospective et Stratégie d'Agglomération Millénaire 3, which was directly linked to the executive, with the aim of supporting reflection on the development of the agglomeration through the creation of a comprehensive area strategy. All the work carried out by Millénaire 3, under the direction of Jacques Moulinier, was aimed at creating a sustainable development strategy for the urban agglomeration, geared toward the pursuit of economic competitiveness and social cohesion, through the involvement of civil society, an area-wide perspective, and a strategic planning exercise.

Barre's strategy fitted the European landscape of strategic planning tools, which are based on multidisciplinarity, the definition of shared objectives, the involvement of different actors, and the integration of expertise and different projects. What differentiated Millénaire 3 from other European strategic plans was a willingness to transform the administrative structure, to broaden consultation, to "ouvrir les fenêtres de la Grand Lyon" (literally "open Grand Lyon's windows") in an ongoing process; it was only partly a planning document. Involvement was not reserved for insiders, but was strongly directed towards the public, civil society, associations, education, and research, and those who were just interested. Communication and publishing occupied a prominent place in Millénaire 3's activities, as did participation in European strategic reflection networks and preparation for days of debate on the issues under discussion in the metropolis. In 2001, at the end of his term of office, Raymond Barre supported the creation of the Development Council, an advisory body made up of representatives of economic, political, and cultural forces, other insiders, officials of institutions, and interested citizens, with the aim of making permanent the path begun by Millénaire 3 with the establishment of an instrument of consultation, debate, and strategic reflection.

Stabilization

The main novelty of the policies inaugurated by Barre lay in the implementation of new frameworks for discussion and negotiation that were capable of involving all the actors in the metropolis in constant interinstitutional cooperation. If Millénaire 3 was the tool used to elaborate projects and publicize them, the Schéma de Développement Economique (SDE), launched in 1997, enabled the definition of an economic development strategy and the involvement of private actors. Openness and external involvement were shared by the SDE and Millénaire 3. The SDE aimed to create the conditions in which partnerships could be built with private actors, opening the debate to noninstitutional players and widening the circle of decision-makers.

In 2001, Gerard Collomb was elected mayor of Lyon and president of COURLY, for the first time with a center-left majority. The alliance between the Socialist Party from which Collomb came and Raymond Barre's center-right UDF (Union for French Democracy), initiated during Barre's term, continued under Collomb. The Socialist Party supported Barre in the Community Council, and Barre granted some COURLY vice-presidential posts to the Socialists. Similarly, the UDF supported Collomb, who had a very narrow majority for election as COURLY president, and Collomb gave vice-presidential posts to right-wing politicians. This is one reason why the concertation tools put in place during Barre's term resisted administrative change. Grand Lyon renewed its commitment to different governance strategies, seeking to increase the city's metropolitan role. The chosen entity to oversee this was again the RUL, which Barre had relaunched as a place for metropolitan area discussions, meetings, and consultation. Collomb invested in the same direction, initiating negotiations with suburban cities to encourage them join forces with Lyon and entrusting the RUL copresidency to the president of the Rhône Alpes region.

The spotlight

While Lyon's success is evidently linked to an institutional commitment that has been quite out of the ordinary, leading the city to be the only one in France to have a properly voted metropolitan area by 2025, after more than two decades of debate and directed actions, it is also true that this success has had some public aspects that are equally relevant to the institutional process.

This is particularly the case with the Fête des Lumières (Festival of Lights), which has grown out of a very old religious tradition to become one of the major tourist attractions as well as a source of local pride.[2] Every year, around December 8 for four days, the city of Lyon is transformed in a popular festival during which light installations curated by the municipality are complemented by those Lyonnais who decorate the facades of their homes with lights. Over the years, the celebration has become an international event that now sees the participation of well-known light artists, has come to engage all the city's neighborhoods, and has even won several awards and prizes. But this is not all.

In a short time, the Fête des Lumières has become a national and international model. It was neighboring Turin, thanks to encouragement from a group of architects headed by Sergio Jaretti, that chose a similar path a decade later: In 1998, at the behest of the then councilor for commerce and city promotion, Fiorenzo Alfieri, the Luci d'artista was born. Lyon and Turin together then gave birth in 2002 to the LUCI (Light Urban Community Association) network, strongly encouraged by Jean Michel Daclin, the councilor for tourism and city promotion who regarded this attraction as a central element of urban policy, along with the theme we will discuss in a moment: food.

LUCI now has more than seventy partner cities, seven of which have won the title of European Capital of Culture, thanks in part to skillful innovation and the good management of urban lighting routes. The network, which touches all continents and all different urban forms, innovates, runs seminars and workshops, and develops best practices. From a diplomatic point of view, this excellent tool has given many Lyon businesses the opportunity to expand their reach, with positive effects both economically and in terms of the city's overall positioning.[3]

In Italy, the Lyon model has also inspired Salerno, which permanently hosts a very appealing and successful festival of lights, blending the tradition of illuminations with the narration of spaces and places. But it

---

[2] On the origins of this festival and the votive tradition that finds expression, see https://en.wikipedia.org/wiki/Festival_of_Lights_(Lyon).

[3] On the subject of urban diplomacy, see Lorenzo Kihlgren Grandi, *City Diplomacy* (London: Palgrave Macmillan, 2020).

is only in the French city that this moment of celebration has begun the widespread curation of urban design through light.

If we look carefully at whether or how the initial ideas have evolved, it appears that Salerno and Turin have both continued with the initial programs; the effect of the events is still only regional in impact, at most. The events in these cities have not been relaunched, and there are no departments within the municipalities to take charge, not only of organization but also research and development—so that more tourists, light artists, and innovators are attracted to the festivals, thereby making the best use of this extraordinary tool.

The 2021 edition of the Fête des Lumières, the first after the pandemic, saw Lyon offer as many as thirty new installations, including ten finalists in a special prize that has been held since 2010: This sees the public engaged in the selection of the displays that are "la plus belle, la plus magique, la plus éblouissainte" ("the most beautiful, the most magical, the most dazzling"). What is surprising is not only the overall quality of the project, but the fact that these works were mostly designed by digital studios operating in Lyon and the region, almost as if (in the manner of a film festival such as the Youth Film Festival in Turin between the 1980s and 1990s, for example) the Fête de Lumières has built a local creative scene, which has become craft and then small industry, and has thus interconnected with the rest of the area's economic and business world.

A final remarkable aspect is that the project has a charitable side as well. Since 2005, the citizens of Lyon have been invited every year to buy a light in the shape of a heart to place on their window, with an extraordinary scenic effect; this purchase supports a local project. The 2021 effort benefited young students who were isolated or in economic difficulties, through the Gaelis Association. This is a concrete example of how an event that promotes the city can become an important social inclusion activity.

Ville lumière, et cuisinière aussi!

In addition to political path-building and communicating urban identity on the basis of a religious tradition that has gradually become a collective passion and pride, involving technological innovation and considerable organization, the city of Lyon has gradually been able to strengthen its image as a tourist destination as well as its social standing by putting to good use two other fundamental intangible assets: cinema and cuisine.

The title of "world capital of gastronomy" has been Lyon's since 1935 thanks to the famous culinary critic Maurice Edmond Sailland, And Lyon was the first city in the world to be filmed. In Paris, on December 28, 1895, the Lumière brothers chose the view of Lyon's Place des Cordeliers as the first city location for their extraordinary invention that would soon change art forever. But it was in the 1980s that this tradition developed, with the foundation of the Institut Lumière in 1982, with the great director and pillar of French cinema Bertrand Tavernier being invited to preside over it. The Institut was established right next to the place where the Lumière brothers had shot their first film. In 2009, the Lyon Film Festival was launched; by its thirteenth year, 2021, there were over 145,000 attendees, including dozens of international guests.

Today, from a production point of view, Lyon is the international headquarters of EuroNews, the only European television network worthy of the name, which for the past few years has found a home in one of the city's completely renovated areas, the island of Confluence, once completely occupied by large industrial enterprises and now totally restored; this is also thanks to the location there of the museum of the same name, inaugurated in 2014, which aims to communicate to citizens and tourists alike more than 3000 years of human history through a rotating display of more than 200,000 objects.

However, the powerful imagery created by Lumière pales into insignificance today in comparison with the engine of contemporary tourism: cuisine. This is a kind of religion that connects very different people and has offered itself as a leading tool for local development in the late 20th and early 21st centuries. This is why Lyon seems to offer in this specific sphere an even more qualified and decisive story than cinema does, even though the latter plays a significant role in the urban imaginary and in the specific cultural and economic activities of many urban communities on the planet (think of Woody Allen's New York, 007's London base, and the renewal of Indian culture with the birth of Bollywood, potentially capable of overshadowing the place from which it takes its name).

Central to Lyon's relationship with cuisine, and its image as the product of tradition, is a specific person: Paul Bocuse.

Lyon's fame dates back to Roman times, when the city of Lugdunum controlled the empire's provincial wine trade. This wine tradition was soon intertwined with the gastronomic tradition, with the great bourgeois families employing in their homes the so-called Mères lyonnaises, excellent cooks who set up their own businesses in the early twentieth century. It was in one of the restaurants born of this tradition, Mère Brazier, that Paul Bocuse, dubbed the "chef of the century," began work. He is the epitome of how an individual can motivate an entire community. With the only restaurant to maintain three Michelin stars for more than fifty consecutive years, Bocuse has inspired not only generations of chefs but also dozens of restaurants; he is linked to an extraordinarily appealing taste offering and to the training of young talent—whose work is the pinnacle of the area's collective identity. Lyon owes a large part of its brand strength to Bocuse, just as Bocuse and the other extraordinary chefs who were born and have lived in the French city have known that they can always count on unique attention from the city, the region, the citizens, and the media; a respect that has also given rise to a world-renowned week of events held in January (usually one of the least interesting months for travel).

Lyon's urban space has become increasingly attractive, and simultaneously a great deal of local pride has been created. Cooking, from being a necessary activity for survival, has become a life-enhancing activity, teaching everyone that quality of life comes from knowing the little things, an attention to detail, and the power of relationships. These messages can be applied far beyond their initial sphere.

Future

Thanks to lights, cinema, and cuisine, Lyon has been able to become the true counterbalance to Paris, to which it is linked by high-speed rail in less than two hours and to which it has previously felt itself inferior. A happy island of balanced and shared development, it now looks with interest at what is happening in its twin Villeurbanne, which began as a dormitory city for immigrants and has been named the "first French capital of culture" for 2022.

As in Pittsburgh, and emblematic also of Brussels—capital of Belgium and seat of the European Union's main governing bodies—Lyon is seeking to extend the positive effects of policies that have transformed its historic center from a place of difficult management and social exclusion into a highly attractive space, to the rest of the city as well. This has meant interventions, as we have seen, along the river corridors but also in former industrial areas, converting them into new educational, cultural, and sports spaces. Of course, the year 2022, despite the roughly 800 events announced, did not deliver all the hoped-for results due to the lingering effects of COVID-19. But the planning was carried over into the following biennium and therefore was not wasted.

In recent years, the new mayor, Grégory Doucet—elected on July 4, 2020, at the head of a strongly ecological coalition—has pursued bold objectives aimed at ensuring the city's role as a protagonist in the twenty-first century, abandoning some old prerogatives and embracing new ones: less meat and more vegetarian options on public and private menus; fewer cars and lower speeds across the metropolitan area (including the pedestrianization of all areas surrounding the city's 206 schools); and a massive reforestation program linked to a complete overhaul of energy models in both private housing and public offices.

The narratives supporting this vision are closely tied to those that have made Anne Hidalgo's approach in Paris successful, particularly in drastically reducing fine-particle pollution (which remains very high in Italy's Po Valley as well as in the metropolitan areas of London and Athens).

Doucet is also waging a battle on gender, giving new momentum to women's presence not only in politics but across the full spectrum of public life. It is a vision he also hopes to reinforce within a key instrument of European urban policy: the Eurocities Assembly, the most powerful and active association of its kind in the continent.

Moreover, as early as 2021, Doucet wrote to then–Prime Minister Jean Castex, urging him to reopen museum spaces that were at risk not only of losing vital resources but also of forfeiting their role as engines of the collective imagination—clearly intending to unite the new environmental vision with a new humanism.

If Lyon succeeds in holding these two elements together, the urban leadership it has enjoyed for the past fifty years will find new ways to assert itself all the way to 2050.

5 Milan
From politics to policies (and back)

A city to drink, but above all to care

When, on February 17, 1992, Mario Chiesa was arrested for corruption in his capacity as president of the Pio Albergo Trivulzio (an ancient retirement home and hospital in Milan), he could never have imagined that almost thirty years later the same place would again become emblematic during the first pandemic that brought the planet to a halt, putting the issue of health care and cure increasingly at the center of social and economic debate.

Born two centuries earlier in a Milan that united enlightened Austro-Hungarian despotism with the activism of the local nobles and bourgeoisie, and the first investor in innovation on the back of events in the Anglo-Saxon world, the Pio Albergo Trivulzio seems to possess a space–time magnetism. It is not far from Santa Maria della Grazie, where visitors from all over the world queue up every day to see Leonardo's Last Supper, or from the San Vittore prison, where many of the protagonists of Tangentopoli spent much of their time under suspicion and then as prisoners.

Crisis

Some people think that Tangentopoli, the first and most important of the urban scandals of the late twentieth century, could only have broken out in Milan, and that thanks to the pool of magistrates involved in *mani pulite*, Milan wanted to react courageously to a phenomenon that was infecting the entire economic life of the city. Events were particularly significant because Milan was viewed as the moral capital of Italy—having been so defined back in 1881 by a Neapolitan admirer of the city, Ruggiero Bonghi, on the occasion of the Italian Industrial Exposition, the second of its kind hosted in the country, after the much smaller one held in Florence twenty years earlier. But what was Milan in 1992? It was the child of the 1980s, having quelled the social clashes of that decade, the one in which the city reached its maximum number of inhabitants and especially in which immigration from the south of the country had peaked. After the great industrial development of the 1950s and 1960s, with steel and rubber production around family dynasties such as the Falck and Pirelli families, the 1980s made Milan Italy's first international city. While Turin was involved in a clash between workers and white-collar workers, and while Rome focused on the forms and rituals of politics, Milan focused on the contemporary—on new spaces on the fringes of the city. These were outside the municipality in the strictest sense, so much so that they took the names Milan 2 and Milan 3, satellite cities built especially for a petit bourgeoisie with great aspirations but without substantial means. The city also developed new functions, with a major focus on services, publishing, and finance.

Milan is the first Italian city to feed off the urban economy: It lives off what it produces, and above all it produces citizens, temporary citizens, who are attracted by the city's new functions and changes in world society. The presence of the Stock Exchange, which in the second half of the 1990s became a SpA (the equivalent of a public limited company), amalgamating the various functions previously spread across the rest of Italy, made Milan into the hub of national finance, and computerization is the prelude to a new generation of the workforce becoming part of an international network. At the same time, the development of Fininvest reinforced by the Mammì Law (passed on August 6, 1990) has strengthened creativity and publishing, of which Milan has been the epicenter since the second half of the 1970s. Around these business polarities universities have been strengthened, with a great development of the private educational sector, Bocconi and Cattolica leading the way. Population density always leads to the development of new services, most notably those related to health care. The link between the press, finance, and those parties that manage growth was not adequately regulated by institutional separation of powers. To do so, in 1992, the judiciary had to intervene.

Relaunch

As the city was not content to maintain an unexceptional profile in Europe and a new springtime for the Milanese economy was desired, it was necessary, despite Milan's historical reluctance to submit to collective strategies, to design a blueprint for the city—as has been written, "not a scheme that everyone must observe, but a design in which everyone moves freely: an idea of Milan."[1]

The industrial mayor and the city factory

There are two possible dates to which we can trace the revitalization of Milan after the image crisis resulting from Tangentopoli.

The first is the 2001 States General, at which Mayor Gabriele Albertini shared the results of his first council term, which had begun in the summer of 1997. This was important for the local community because of the participation of significant figures from the worlds of business, culture, media, academia, and religion.

On a national and global level, the communicative relaunch certainly coincided with the awarding of the 2015 Expo, strongly desired by the city's first female mayor, Letizia Moratti, in agreement with Prime Minister Romano Prodi, and achieved thanks to a team of experts working in the field of bids and management of major events, such as Paolo Glisenti and Roberto Daneo, as well as a team of architects of world renown, including Stefano Boeri, Richard Burdett, and Jacques Herzog.

These two events are really two sides of the same coin. A coin made of a precious material for cities seeking their future: managerialism and a relative independence from politics, understood as a system of relationships that impose actions that are incompatible not only with laws but also, and above all, with the needs of citizens.

The story of Gabriele Albertini and Letizia Moratti is in this sense associated with their two chief executives, Stefano Parisi and Giuseppe Sala, who, not surprisingly, almost two decades after serving as "head of the business" in Italy's second most important municipality, have in turn

---

[1] Assessorato allo Sviluppo del territorio, Comune di Milano, *Ricostruire la Grande Milano, Documento di Inquadramento delle politiche urbanistiche comunali*, June 2000.

challenged each other to become mayor, without major ideological differences but only with a different form of notoriety and credibility with the electorate.

When Silvio Berlusconi asked Gabriele Albertini to run as first citizen for a center-right coalition led by Forza Italia in 1997, the potential new politician had no connection whatsoever with the history of Italian parties. He was an entrepreneur who—despite youthful yearnings to become a magistrate, which bound him amicably to Milan's chief prosecutor, Francesco Saverio Borrelli—had his work cut out for him as head of the family business and as president of Federmeccanica, a role that made him credible in the eyes of all those who hoped for a concrete revitalization of the Lombard capital. The family business was in the northeastern part of the hinterland, close to Monza Park; and Albertini had an almost unwavering faith in development but especially in industrial-style organization. It is no coincidence that he put at the center of his work as mayor a total rethinking of the corporate form of the municipality, with functions shifting from being strictly vertical to decidedly horizontal, as envisaged by the Bassanini reform, with a mandate given to politics in terms of direction, control, and monitoring, and an active and responsible role assigned to the administration's top employees. Parisi was able to motivate his executives with rewards that were previously completely absent in the public administration. Public Milan, which had seemed either to hold back or even thwart local development, once again became a second fundamental driving force of entrepreneurial Milan—but neither seemed to want to take over from the other, as had happened in the 1970s and 1980s, with ideological clashes being the result.

Albertini worked on dozens of "dormant" dossiers, particularly those concerning the privatization of many of Milan City Council's investee companies, and together with Parisi he initiated a huge speed-up on the city's internet cabling, creating a new company, Fastweb, which soon became a benchmark for relations between public entity and private enterprise. Thanks to his operational vision, the mayor was also able to combine this with an uncommon ability to listen to the citizenry, who were involved in a very broad search for information. Albertini addressed a letter to all the Milanese that contained twenty-three questions in which he requested that they express their opinions but also their willingness to collaborate for the future of the community. There were over 200,000 responses, thus refuting the many, especially from within the city council itself, who thought the initiative was completely useless, indeed counterproductive. At this time the political divide between the media and the citizenry had reached an all-time high, but Albertini received even greater approval than that derived from the vote that had brought him to office: 69 percent of respondents considered that life in Milan had definitely improved since the industrialist took office in Palazzo Marino, the seat of the City Council in Piazza della Scala, while only 13 percent considered it to have worsened; the remainder saw no significant difference.

During his second term, Albertini laid the foundations for a Milan "host city," one that was capable of hosting major events. He relaunched the role of the Triennale, which under the presidency of Davide Rampello once again became one of Milan's cultural and creative engines. This acceleration toward Milan's reinvention as a city of events was emphasized by the decision to greatly enhance the trade fair system: This gave rise to the new Rho Fiera hub, designed by Massimiliano Fuksas and inaugurated in 2005, to complement the historic Fiera, which was founded in 1923, upgraded in the first half of the 1990s, and is now the site mainly used for large international congresses.

Although alongside this infrastructure for major events, the themes of fashion and design are strengthening, Milan is not yet a world-class city because it is not perceived as a place of cultural production and innovation in all sectors. However, it is ready to become one. What is needed is a major catalyzing event that is capable of making people understand the expansion plan that Albertini and Parisi have envisioned, and of addressing Milan's alleged decline in the face of the simultaneous rise of two cities against which it has often been pitted: Rome and Turin.

Rome, not accepting its role as an exclusively political capital, also wants to be reborn around its great beauty, and has used the Great Jubilee of 2000 to clean up its streets and buildings. Thanks to the charisma of two mayors, Rutelli and Veltroni, it has launched new events based on subjects that have been traditionally the preserve of the north of the country: a film festival (competing with Venice) and a fashion week (competing with Milan).

Turin, meanwhile, which is less than 150 kilometers from Milan (the travel time soon to be shortened thanks to the Frecciarossa), has been eroding the historic popularity of the Lombard capital, taking from it the title of world capital of design and fending off those Milanese who want to bring the Book Fair back to the shadow of the Madonnina. Turin is so competitive that after hosting the Olympics it also asked for the Expo venue for 2015. But Romano Prodi thought the opportunity would be more interesting for Milan, and on October 26, 2006, he sat down next to Letizia Moratti, former president of RAI and minister of education and research from 2001 to 2005, who had been the new mayor of Milan for a few months, to announce the city's next great challenge: to host the world's largest event, the Universal Exposition, next to the world's largest exhibition space, that of Rho.

The title chosen for the event, overseen by the design talent of Roberto Daneo, formerly an assistant to Turin Mayor Valentino Castellani in building the solid international relations that got the 2006 Turin Winter Olympics off the ground, was "Feeding the Planet—Energy for Life." This intertwined a typically Italian theme and at that time one of great topicality and popularity, food, with the great SDGs of the United Nations. Milan, to become a truly global city and compete internationally with such world centers as London and Barcelona, Shanghai and Singapore, Boston and Lyon, had to show that it was capable not only of improving the performance of its administration, but also of becoming a global platform for renewal.

So, just over ten years after it had lost its central role and become primarily known as a city of political malfeasance, Milan reacted strongly, and a hundred years after hosting the 1906 World's Fair, which brought to Italy the theme of large-scale infrastructure links and celebrated the construction of the Simplon tunnel, appointed another manager, this time a woman who was committed to social work; someone who was from a Genoese family but was part of a group that had strong international connections, an expert in state administration and large investments. Moratti was made mayor, and also an ambassador for the excellence of the city—and more generally of Italy.

An ambassador for the world city

With Letizia Moratti, Italy returned to cheer on Milan. She was aided by intellectual figures such as Stefano Boeri, an architect from a noble Milanese family, who was linked to the best names in design and also to economic and social thought around the world—and a student and personal friend of Rem Koolhaas, in turn one of the most influential world figures in the field of urban imagination. Boeri, at the request of Moratti, together with the very high-profile thinker Ricky Burdett, who was also appointed director of a Venice Architecture Biennial at this time, proposed an Expo that would be dedicated not to the wealth of Western peoples, but to the expansion and growth of developing countries, thanks to whose votes (and especially their moral support) Milan could win the race to host the 2015 Expo.

Boeri began by proposing a model of "urban biodiversity" that would be applied to the Expo. This would be designed as an ideal Roman city, centered on a *cardo* (a north–south street) and a *decumanus* (an east–west street), with all the states having pavilions of the same square footage. Above all, the site was imagined as a large garden at the western gates of Milan, redeveloping an area, Rho Pero, that for decades had housed the most polluting refineries, the borders of a city that looked more to Genoa than to Turin, being almost an offshoot of the northwestern hinterlands. In Boeri's proposal, officially presented on April 26, 2010, Milan would build a large garden, a new-generation urban agricultural plot, capable of producing for the city as much as it needed and indeed even more, to contribute to the general sustainability of the planet, emphasizing the different relationship required between man, land consumption, food, and its distribution.

These were also the years in which the "good, clean, and fair" concept of Carlo Petrini, the name behind Slow Food, was popularized. His goal was to draw a contrast with fast food, which appeared, perhaps not coincidentally, for the first time in Italy in the Milan of the 1980s. Petrini, who launched the first Salone del Gusto in Turin in 1996, has since 2004 associated with his movement an even more important event from the point of view of global politics: Terra Madre. A large gathering of producers committed to biodiversity, this broadened the focus from the quality of the products to the quality of the planet, through an insistence on good practices, on the need to keep as many species alive as possible, and doing so by giving agriculture a new role and workers in the sector wages more in keeping with the strategic value of their daily actions.

Milan thus became the paradoxical site of the clash between big finance and the new ideas that were about to explode into the 21st century. With the candidacy as Expo venue first and with the realization of the project later, Milan was the mirror—for better or for worse—of everything that was becoming fundamental for the survival of the planet, but also of the new challenges that Italy had to take on to play a new role in Europe and the world.

Expo or no Expo? All for Expo, Milan for one

Milan made it: May 1, 2015 was the opening day of Expo. It seemed impossible, given the area to be prepared, the potent economic interests that intersected with political and organizational choices. Italy, since Rome 1960 (and except Turin 2006), had never really been able to take advantage of a major event at all levels, and to be appreciated for it at a global level. But this time the success was great and tangible, and the benefits to the city were obvious. Let us quickly review the steps by which this came about.

The decision about the World Expo venue had been announced on March 31, 2008: Milan beat Smyrna eighty-six votes to sixty-one. But the marathon had just begun; beating the Turks would prove to be the easiest part of Moratti's tenure. This is a story that often repeats itself: If you need to unite against another party, it is not too difficult to team up, even for the Italians, who are not exactly naturals at working together. But as soon as you win, then you have to decide who the project leader is. It would seem to be clear that the mayor would coordinate specific activities to accomplish what was promised in the bid, following the plan as closely as possible; the region would broaden the focus to include infrastructure and the involvement of neighboring territories; while the state would use the event for international promotion, coordinating business delegations according to the interests at stake. All this would take place with the same players as before at both regional and national levels, with a natural turnover of businesses involved when necessary.

This happens in France; in Germany; maybe even in Spain. But in Italy, no. Each time it is necessary to start all over again: to recontract, rebuild governance, redefine objectives. In Italy there are always two teams, those for whom nothing ever goes right and those who overcome every obstacle even at the cost of very high and somewhat unjustified personal risks.

After getting the Expo, the controversy began. Who should run it, with what skills, with what goals? A big event is often an extraordinary opportunity to highlight a series of ongoing transformations, or alternatively to keep everyone from noticing something else that is happening and is not considered vital or desirable for people to focus on. The case of the World Cup in Argentina is among the most exemplary: A dictatorship at the height of its crimes let the world into its own house, and the resulting narrative was almost all positive.

In the case of Expo 2015, the true urban transformation of Milan, the one set in motion by Albertini by uprooting the old way of doing things and setting in motion a path to international investment that produced the redevelopment of the entire area near the Porta Garibaldi station, from the Varesine to the Isola, as well as the City Life project and the rethinking of the old Fiera, was almost deliberately overshadowed by a temporary transformation of the fish-shaped area between the railway, the Bollate prison, and the large Post Office sorting center.

The decision to allocate this area for the Expo was not particularly rational from the point of view of future urban development. Behind it, for example, there was no coordination with Turin—not even when the connection between Caselle and Malpensa airports could have been planned with a small high-speed extension, maybe by using part of the remaining Olympic funds: About 70 million euro not spent on the event could have made the infrastructural and thus the economic relationship between the two cities even more intertwined and positive.

The projects that have involved the two capitals over the years, prompted by the Turin Department of Culture and strengthened by the soft link between the two Chambers of Commerce, included a great classical music festival, MI-TO SettembreMusica, its name combining the historic SettembreMusica brand (an event launched in Turin in the late 1970s with the aim of bringing people out of the sadness and isolation into which they had plunged during a period of political violence and social upheaval known as the Years of Lead) with a simple and understandable acronym; and the promotion of the integration of two excellent universities, creating the Alta Scuola Politecnica for contemporary art and design. However, these did not succeed in bringing about any further joint action. In the end, Milan snubbed Turin, taking the best of what the Savoy city could offer: these were the Banca San Paolo, which became Intesa Sanpaolo with a governance and management strongly centered on Milan, and a focus on music and contemporary art culture of which Turin was the root but Milan, thanks to its large private market, the natural destination for the public.

These agreements about content did not bring about a planning of shared areas. This was not the case with the Expo area, despite the fact that it was in the western quadrant of the Lombard capital, less than half an hour by high-speed train from Turin. It also did not happen when Turin began to discuss, and then choose, the area in which to create its own city of health, a gamble based on the Pittsburgh model: This has run aground not only thanks to the quibbles of bureaucracy, but also because of the needs of the local health organizations, which have always been accustomed to working (and therefore also living) in the area south of the city, towards the Langhe and Liguria. This was even though the so-called Scalo Vanchiglia could have been chosen, which would have brought Milan and Turin even closer together, perhaps in agreement with Novara, a very important center from the point of view of biomedical research and production, always been linked to Lombardy even though it is the last offshoot of eastern Piedmont.

There has been much debate about the Expo areas—their value and the best way to manage them (buying and selling, buying and managing, renting and returning, and so on—but perhaps there has been too little discussion about the interrelation between different areas, the content of the Expo project, and its value for the country as a whole.

Before going on to look at some data from the event itself, and on its extraordinary and in some ways unexpected success, let us compare Expo 2015 with what Barcelona did in 2004 with the Forum of Cultures and London did with the 2012 Olympics. Difficult urban areas, preexisting neighborhoods with a complicated destiny, were reinvented as destinations capable of enlarging the urban perimeter, a new mechanism that was capable of aggregating an impressive number of visitors, thanks to the availability of new convention centers and business and sports parks immediately after the event.

For Expo, and for Milan, this role was taken not by the area in which the event took place, but by other areas that were undergoing transformation in parallel. The perceived beneficial effects of Expo, which were well orchestrated from the point of view of public communication, were linked above all to the availability—thanks to the event—of new public urban areas, such as Piazza Gae Aulenti, the new center of an urban imagery which in turn has produced a large park, overlooked by Stefano Boeri's Bosco Verticale—which has become the true icon of Expo, more so than the Tree of Life.

The orange redemption

Paradox within a paradox: Similar to this—with the political roles reversed—was the Matera 2019 affair. The city won the title of European Capital of Culture, but the center-left mayor lost the elections immediately following the win. In Milan, the capacity for international relations brought about by the Moratti administration and the winning of Expo did not convince the Milanese citizens who were called to vote in 2011; instead they rewarded a completely different city project. This was the creation of a city in which the common good was to prevail, with the promise of an inclusive, participatory, green, and equal community—watchwords that were not, if we look at history as a whole, so far removed from the principles that had inspired the Expo bid. As had already happened with the Forum of Culture in Barcelona, the final act of a very long socialist political trajectory, the mayor's leadership had linked the development of the city itself to these extreme consequences. Many observers tended to emphasize the economic interest groups behind these activities. Personally, having been involved in much local development action, I am not much into conspiracy theories; rather, I have learnt that there are competing logics, in which personal histories, vested interests, and contextual tendencies are intertwined—which in a democratic system leads to choices and effects that are by no means predictable. We are obliged in urban space, in its democratic complexity, to accept a certain serendipity. In recent years, this must be contextualized in a polarization of choices.

In the case of Milan, the question is whether the ongoing urban transformations would have had the same prominence and credibility. Have these transformations brought more wealth or more relative poverty? Have they set in motion a path of greater inequality than if the transformations had not occurred? Or do we have to strictly separate the two issues, and on the one hand say that we do not want transformations, we do not want more land consumption (in the case of Milan, many of these areas were already in use—so it was reuse that happened)?

The request for more democracy, more transparency, fewer ties with the "strong powers" (always denied by Albertini), the need to imagine a new Milan beyond the new physical settlements and beyond the rhetoric behind Expo meant that Giuliano Pisapia was an ideal candidate to challenge Letizia Moratti, much more so than Stefano Boeri, his competitor in the primaries, who was perceived as connected to a certain part of Milan that people wanted to finally put in the minority. Stefano Rolando, professor of political communication at the IULM in Milan, and author of an important book with Pisapia,[2] who headed the Brand Milan Committee from 2012 to 2017, summarized why Pisapia became mayor. It seems appropriate to report these ten reasons in detail:

1. Pisapia brilliantly anticipated and benefited from the general trend in Europe whereby citizens, having the opportunity to vote, choose to punish the government if a crisis continues.
2. Not being a party member, Pisapia accepted the party–corporate pact, ensuring autonomy of choice. Letizia Moratti took, because of insecurity, the opposite path, abandoning her independent position and bowing to the parties in her coalition.
3. He encouraged bottom-up and widespread communication in reaction to the coarse and often vulgar aspects of the campaigning of the parties formerly in the majority in Milan (at its climax, Moratti was falsely accused of having been a car thief), thus fueling a rare strand in Italian political communication: humor.
4. Pisapia used the expression "gentle force," referring to the vital demands made by young people and especially women.
5. Creating the budget involved broad participation by the political network, marking an innovative and creative step in Italian electoral communication.
6. The idea that the essential forum for political communication, whether on the periphery of Milan or at its heart, was the city and not the media was grasped and encouraged.
7. Once Pisapia had ensured the loyalty of all left-oriented parties, he favored the progressive enlargement of alliances, aggregating secular and Catholic groupings that tended toward the center, by virtue of a guarantee that had been made when he beat the PD as an outsider in the primaries.
8. He resurrected "reformism" in Milan by making carefully selected references (Greppi, Pertini, Pellizza da Volpedo).
9. He resurrected the 'democratic' membership of Catholics by mak-

[2] Giuliano Pisapia, Stefano Rolando, *Due arcobaleni nel cielo di Milano (e altre storie). Dialogo su Milano e l'Italia* (Milan: Bompiani, 2011).

ing carefully selected references (Tettamanzi, Don Giussani, Don Milani).

10. He interpreted the historical mission of political communication as having a story to tell (and he did this by making it clear that Letizia Moratti did not have a story to tell).

As can be seen, at no point did Pisapia directly address the Expo issue—which already dominated and would continue to dominate the media scene for the following four years.

Was Expo, for most citizens, experienced as a tax or as an opportunity? Answering this question is not necessarily related to reality; rather, what counts is not just the need of citizens to actively participate and reflect on the necessary daily activities regarding the transformations of the place in which they live, but also their desire to have fun, to feel part of a larger world, to gain relief from everyday life. From afar, our advanced cities look a lot like ancient Greek and Roman cities, where people waited for the Olympic Games precisely so they could take a break, get together, and complete projects that would last for generations.

For a certain period, Pisapia distanced himself from Expo, using the event at most as a soft power that helped to build or strengthen international relations. Then he had to give in to the evidence; to assign importance to something he did not believe in. At the opening ceremony, he said: "We made it, Milan has woken up and it is a beautiful first of May. Expo was born and lives to speak to the whole of mankind: To say that inequality is not invincible, Milan offers all of itself in this game."

Beyond politics, beyond the city: Expo as a social fact and as an engine of communication

In this city that offers itself to the world and seduces it, there are still critics, even those who on May 1 fought against Expo even when it was already open; but there are also those who wanted to take all the opportunities that Expo could generate at a local level, strengthening the identity of the host city and above all allowing Expo to become a common language, a thread that was able to unite the country (one of the tasks of the Italian Pavilion, the place deputed to represent the best of everything inside Expo). Among these optimists, two are worth mentioning for the work they did and the impact that work had: Giacomo Biraghi and Stefano Mirti.

Giacomo Biraghi, who for a long time served the Milanese chamber system, helped to create the birth of messaging that operated in parallel to official communications, strongly autonomous, but not conflicting with, but rather strongly consistent with, the original ideas of the Expo candidacy. His vision also built a series of parallel events with a simple but significant title: Expo in the City. This was a ploy not only to attract more sponsors and to spread the message more widely, but also to emphasize and explain Expo's broader mission, which was to make Milan not just a business destination, a place where one could enjoy the enhanced heritage, but above all a city where one can feel like a citizen, even if only for a weekend or a few weeks—a city to look forward to and miss when one wasn't there.

Stefano Mirti, architect, designer, and digital communication expert, a former lecturer at the Interaction Design Institute in Ivrea and then at Naba (the New Academy of Fine Arts in Milan and Rome), was the digital communication coordinator for Expo. He came up with the idea of "hacking" Expo, not organizing communication in a top-down manner, but rather rolling the event into the web, multiplying the effect of messaging from below and transforming it into a collective narrative.

These two experiences broadened the base of Expo: They made it into the first universal exhibition involving the digital society in a city that was finally proud of its beauty. Is it possible to accept this experience? In twenty years, Milan has become more beautiful—not only those places that have been reborn through the urban transformations that have taken place, but also in many smaller areas, which have been able to network and integrate themselves into a region that has greatly improved in terms of aesthetics. Cities such as Brescia and Bergamo, not to mention the more obvious Cremona and Mantua, have focused on urban quality as a distinctive and attractive element. From the 1950s to the 1980s, Milan was a place of work, business, exchange, and even higher education. After Expo, it has become a place of contemplation, reflection, of not only free but also liberated time; a city in which parks are now even more important than bus lanes, pedestrianized spaces have been reclaimed for young and old, and with many new central focal points, such as those around Porta Genova or the so-called Zona Tortona, the reinforcement of Bicocca not only thanks to the university and Hangar Bicocca but also to dozens of start-ups that have settled in the area; a city that, similarly to Barcelona and also Lyon, does not impose traditional municipal boundaries. Milan has become the umbrella name for a large urban area that needs new political integration, since social and economic integration has already taken hold. Expo, not by chance, was held outside Milan, in Rho Pero, and brought millions of people to the borders of the periurban area, where the railway crosses the last stations of the Milanese metro, pushing the citizens' desire to seek new spaces on the edges—essentially inventing them.

But if Expo had an impact on places, it obviously had an even greater impact on relationships—we are talking here above all about positive relationships. The success of Expo has given confidence, courage, and pride, among all the city's inhabitants. It has rebuilt a social capital that has become one with the new brand of the city, which no one has been able to oppose, whatever their initial opinion.

Stabilization

Unlike the Olympics and other sporting events, which, having landed in a chosen candidate city, bring it to life and create a great media impact, an Expo traditionally falls into the category of mega-events, such as the European Capitals of Culture, and not into the category of media events, such as the Olympics, Formula 1, or the football World Cup.

Both Milan, with the Expo, and Matera, with the Capital of Culture, were able to relaunch events thanks to the use of social media, but also thanks to a new interest in cultural and tourist Italy, one for the north of the country and the other for the south.

Thus, the success with the public has allowed Expo to relaunch a more historical and intimate account of Milan, not only that of fashion and design, but also that of history and food. These more human themes are closer to most people, and have made Milan not only more appealing, thanks to the work of so many people working in the cultural sector, led first by Stefano Boeri and then by Filippo Del Corno, councilors and coordinators of long-term projects, but also more appreciated by the inhabitants themselves, who have mingled with visitors from all over the world. The number of those who bought tickets increased from May to October, so much so that at one point it seemed that Expo would be able to stay open beyond the six months allowed and agreed with the Bureau International des Expositions.

Winning this gamble brought a dowry of credibility and visibility to the Commissioner General of Expo, Beppe Sala, formerly Director General of the Milan municipality under Letizia Moratti, and a long-standing manager trained in the world of telecommunications. He was identified as the best candidate to replace a mayor, Giuliano Pisapia, who, however beloved, decided not to continue his political challenge in that role, but to take on a mandate more in keeping with his skills, not the executive ones that belong to mayors, but broad moral and political direction; he had national and even European aspirations.

Sala ran in the primaries, the same primaries that crowned Pisapia as mayoral candidate against Moratti in 2011. In that case, 68,000 people voted; in 2016, 60,000 Milanese citizens chose their ideal mayor. Sala beat center-right candidate Stefano Parisi in the runoff. Both managers in the world of telecommunications, both former general managers of the municipality, they both supported the idea that Milan is a city of doing, and were not interested in a theoretical discussion about the future of the city. Sala—contrary to what might have been expected, but as a good manager—immediately set out to work not on the city's strengths (to which he had made a strong contribution as CEO of Expo SpA and as sole commissioner of the event), but on its weaknesses: inclusion, suburbs, new social vocations. If the economy is going well, if tourism is flourishing and not only brings representatives of companies to Milan for trade fairs or congresses, but also attracts citizens from all over the world who would like not only to visit but also to live in the city, the mayor has the task of being like Achilles with the tortoise: to understand in which direction the city is moving and try to reach it.

Future

On closer inspection, therefore, Milan has been able to enhance the joint work of Albertini and Moratti without publicly contradicting it, even on the part of those who came later and were elected in clear ideological opposition to the city that had been envisioned by the center-right (only Pisapia proposed a different path in his candidacy, but failed to implement it). In twenty years, between 1997 and 2016, the city gave rise to dozens of new initiatives, demonstrating that it is the true driving force behind the Italian system. While Turin took advantage of the Olympics and, with its first strategic plan, promoted a temporary repositioning of its image, which did not, however, translate into a new model of urban growth; and while Rome has exploited the charisma of the two mayors Rutelli and Veltroni to relaunch it as a beautiful tourist destination, but has failed to give continuity to the relaunch either at the level of infrastructure or at the level of widespread urban quality; Milan has succeeded in giving itself a medium- to long-term plan with an operational capacity and a constant public–private partnership.

Growth was put on hold by the pandemic, which had a devastating effect across Lombardy and even cast doubt on whether Milan's urban system could still serve as a driver of the national economy. That fear, however, did not come true. Between 2022 and 2025, Milan's growth was steady, fueled by ever-increasing investment and attractiveness, with a positive narrative also tied to the upcoming Winter Olympics scheduled for February 6–22, 2026. Beyond the successful urban transformations of Porta Garibaldi and the Varesine areas, notable progress has been seen in more peripheral districts as well, thanks both to the arrival of new international firms establishing headquarters and to the impact of new university campuses—such as the Politecnico in Bovisa and the Bicocca University campus. These have not only attracted talent but also significantly pushed up average property prices per square meter, saturated the rental market, and driven up costs, both for the thousands of Italian and foreign students enrolled in Milan's numerous universities and for the many workers employed in essential personal services, who must increasingly live far from where they work.

This situation is not unusual; it combines the well-known effects of gentrification with a touch of overtourism, adding positive elements (the city's recognized attractiveness in higher education and the perception of a qualified labor market) to less "noble" ones, such as the financialization of urban planning and, at the same time, salaries that are not high enough. The latter point is especially relevant to current debates: in Italy, wages are on average much lower, while prices are still relatively modest, which makes it easier for outsiders to spend—whether as tourists or as investors.

Milan, though it has managed to accelerate its growth thanks to ad hoc structures (such as *Yes Milano*) and to increase both temporary and permanent residents, has failed to balance this growth with greater attention to disadvantaged groups. As always, relying on a single model does not make cities stronger, but weaker. Thus, since the end of the pandemic, Milan—also a capital of music, both produced (as the historic home of major international groups blended with national brands such as Sony, Universal, and BMG) and performed (with new trends like trap music emerging from the city's outskirts, especially Rozzano, home to many of Italy's new rappers, whose lyrics and lifestyles hardly promote a gentle or sustainable model of existence)—has faced increasingly widespread urban violence. This has sparked public debates and attempts at new policies, especially to protect women and young girls, who have reported growing unease and threats in parks and around railway hubs due to organized youth gangs. But these efforts have not generated a new idea of the city, which has instead slid into one of the defining ills of our time: polarization in living as well as in communication.

Milan has become at once richer and poorer, more desired and more criticized. The 2026 Olympics—initially seen as a further relaunch after the success of Expo 2015—have gradually become just another event, with no real public discussion on what their legacy should or could be. Yet the Olympics in general, and the Paralympics in particular (whose movement has grown strongly in the last three summer and winter editions), could provide not only a celebration of sport as the ultimate moment of cohesion across diverse groups, but also an occasion for encounter and new visions of the future. Moreover, thanks to the Olympic masterplan and the construction of athletes' villages, Milan will gain thousands of new beds for young people, which could lower per capita housing costs for those who want to study in the city.

Will it happen? So far, there are no signs. Instead of recognizing that debate is a positive act and that finding new solutions—not just for the host city but also in the name of a global community—would be a result of extraordinary importance, the February 2026 Games are conceived merely as a grand parade. They will no doubt succeed, given the quality of the organizers, but risk leaving nothing in citizens' hearts—least of all that beautiful pride in helping to improve everyone's life.

This idea of Milan as "a city for the few"—entirely false (a clearer reading of cohesion and inclusion investment data from an important player like the Cariplo Foundation would suffice)—is now being called into question. A recent investigation by the Milan judiciary has raised doubts not only about administrative actions that may have unduly favored developers and architects involved in the city's most important urban transformations of the past fifteen years (among them Coima and Stefano Boeri), but, above all, about the very model of the city: a city without real politics, reduced to a mere instrument of economic growth rather than redistribution, and without a cultural vision except insofar as it allows small groups to speculate on the collective interest.

This is a vision I personally do not share at all, yet it has quickly taken root, echoing the theses put forward by Lucia Tozzi in her book *L'invenzione di Milano.* To me it seems that if urban demography is an inescapable sign of positive development, then a Milan that reached the milestone of 1.4 million citizens in 2022 has shown that it has risen to the challenge of entering the new millennium. But at what cost?

Perhaps the long delay in deciding to become a city of 4 million—a true metropolitan city—is now costing it more than ever. Only by imagining a greater Milan, with quality services for all, sustainable costs, adequate salaries, and a rail link like Trenord's suburban line, which too often seems left to its own devices yet represents a unique and extraordinary potential if genuinely integrated with Metropolitana Milanese (wouldn't it finally make sense for them to be a single company?), can the city move forward.

In my view, the point is not to repudiate everything Milan has achieved, but to rebalance it—not with a pointless battle over city models (with or without skyscrapers, with or without tourists, with or without out-of-town students), but with collective growth policies that have always been part of the city's DNA. These policies have not been betrayed in practice but have rather been sidelined in the priorities of the leadership.

Once again, Milan leads Italy in an international conversation—but one that would be better served by avant-garde thinking, not visions rooted in a past that truly no one longs to return to.

6 Istanbul
Crossroads or monad?

The capital of nationalist cosmopolitanism

> "The building of a strong Europe is not an attempt to build a new empire, but an endeavor to end, once and for all, the age of empires. [...] Were Europe to have a common seat and thus a stronger voice in the United Nations, for example, the European voice could call for strengthening international institutions and the application of international law. Europe should encourage and support similar moves toward improved cooperation in and among Asia, Latin America, and Africa, promoting a vision of a world integrated for the common good, rather than one divided into antagonistic geopolitical blocs."

When Kemal Dervis, minister of the economy in the Turkish government between 2001 and 2002, wrote these words, it was early 2005. For ten years, the capital of his country, Ankara, had been working to join the European Union. After the crisis of 1999, caused by the terrible earthquake in Izmit, the nation had been able to recover and take advantage of what Dervis called good globalization.

Turkey, founded as a republic in 1923 by Mustafa Kemal Atatürk, was becoming one of good globalization's symbols. It was ratifying the European Constitution in Rome, waiting for the EU member states to welcome it in 2009 as part of a project that must see what Joseph Nye calls "soft power" prevail.

An example of this exceptional opportunity is the former capital, Istanbul. It was Atatürk himself who wanted to build a new city in the heart of Anatolia to give greater stability to a secular state that could have been torn apart by religious strife from the start; but Byzantium/Constantinople/Istanbul is the whole of Turkey at least as much as Paris is the whole of France.

On the other hand, Turkey's pro-European vocation stems from 3 percent of its geographical area, all of which is located within the municipal boundaries of one of the most fascinating cities in the world, one that has always been at the heart of trade, knowledge, debate, and artistic and scientific innovation. A metropolis whose mayor from 1994 to 1999 was a certain Recep Erdoğan, who realized that his city's land was extraordinarily valuable, and carefully and skillfully sold it to businessmen from the Middle East. With their money he was able to stabilize his party's power and make it an inescapable driving force in Turkish politics.

While Erdoğan worked on a new nation project, Kadir Topbaş became mayor in 2004, and remained in post until 2017: He is the politician who has governed the city on the Bosporus for the longest time (there has been a mayor in Istanbul for just under a century). Under his tenure, some of the most important contemporary ambitions of this Euro-Asian metropolis were tested and partly implemented. Above all, there was incredible development in all areas of urban life, so much so that there follows a detailed analysis of the opportunities created and those that have been lost owing to national and international circumstances.

It is these historical traits that make Istanbul one of the most important and interesting cities in the world at the beginning of the 21st century.

Crisis

The end of the European dream

Istanbul, and with it the whole of Turkey, has always had a European spirit. This is not only because the Turkish coastline was Greek for centuries, and that ideas, philosophies, and myths were born there that nourished the image and identity of the entire continent; it is not only because Atatürk set in motion and took definitive steps to resemble the great nations of the Old Continent; but it is also because networks, both economic and recreational, have made the great city on the Bosporus a point of reference.

There are three primary sectors: industrial production, which began with the automotive and interior design sectors; sports, with the constant presence of Turkish teams in all European competitions; and culture, with a continuous dialogue between intellectual, literary, and artistic production, the result of endless mutual influences.

In 1969, Tofaş (the Türk Otomobil Fabrikası Anonim Şirketi, or the Turkish Automobile Factory) was founded in Istanbul's industrial suburbs, and was for a long time the first and largest car manufacturer in Asia. It was born out of a partnership with FIAT that was promoted by Vehbi Kos, and has a large production facility in Bursa, in which in its first year, 1971, some 40,000 cars were produced annually; today it is able to put ten times as many—some 450,000—on the market every year. The first time I arrived at the train station in Istanbul, in 1985, I was surrounded by yellow and black taxis that made me feel as if I was at home in Turin: They were identical to the FIAT 131, even though they were called the Tofaş Murat—later slowly replaced by the FIAT Uno, Palio, and Tipo (which is still produced there today in a completely revamped version).

As was often the case in urban areas, from Paris to Cologne, from Turin to Nagoya, this central form of industrial automobile production greatly influenced the entire metropolitan system, not only at the level of imagery (even more than in the West, the car in Istanbul and the whole of Turkey meant freedom of action and expression for the few who could own one), but also in terms of urban space management. The traffic jams in the big metropolises in the 1980s and the 1990s became the leitmotif of the local lifestyle, forcing everyone to organize their day around the queues of urban commuters. It was Erdoğan himself who found an initial solution to the major problems caused by the thousands of cars in the narrow streets of the city center, and also along the Bosporus routes: He completely renovated the public bus fleet and provided concrete and low-cost answers to the demand for mobility that emerged in the early 1990s. At the same time, he had the intuition that he had to work on the waste collection system, transforming the metropolitan area of Istanbul just in time by applying Teutonic-style best practice, rather than abandoning it to become an impracticable jumble of slums, as was the case in Mexico City, Mumbai, and other cities of the so-called Third World, which seemed destined only to perpetuate a cycle of poverty for most of their inhabitants.

These were the same years in which Istanbul's football and basketball teams climbed the rankings of their respective European categories, taking Turkish sport to the top of individual competitions, attracting more and more spectators, and giving rise to the demand for new stadiums. Population growth went hand in hand with a new income regime, the traditional bourgeoisie living in the city center invested in new residential areas, and rich Turkish emigrants returned to invest in the city they had left thirty, forty, in some cases fifty years earlier—to move mainly to Germany. The Prussian regime had in some ways been Atatürk's model, and relations between the first Turkish and German universities were very strong; but a strong relationship was also in place with the US world, where the ruling classes of the 1970s and 1980s were largely formed. Indeed, we must remember that for a long time Turkey was the main NATO base against Russian expansionism during the Cold War.

In the second part of the 1990s, having overcome an initial economic crisis, a new industrial season opened in Istanbul; this profits much more consciously from relocation. Local entrepreneurs can manufacture high-quality products and compete on important international markets, especially in the furniture sector, and a kitchen and living room district competes and cooperates with Italian regions such as Marche and Puglia. These sectors are obviously aided by demographic and economic growth in the region, by the birth of new autonomous banks and by a relationship with the Middle Eastern world, which is intensifying and which, as we shall see later, provided Erdoğan, first mayor and then prime minister, with substantial funds from the capital gains of the oil market to invest in large new urban spaces.

These were the years—between 1985 and 2000—in which Istanbul doubled its population, offered great educational opportunities to many of its young people, and became the driving force behind a new tourist offer that connected the urban dimension and the extraordinary architectural heritage of eighteen centuries of historical centrality, from the Greeks to the Romans to the Byzantine and Ottoman empires, to a world that seemed to be able to grow without limits, and that seemed to be able to westernize without falling into the clash of civilizations prophesied by Huntington. A product that is associated with the rest of Turkey, made up of the sea on the one hand (in the old Greek colonies, along the coast of Izmir and Pergamon), but above all surprising inland areas, such as Cappadocia, which in a short time became a destination to be placed side by side with the Byzantium that once was. The growth in exports and tourism is associated with a powerful demand for infrastructure: In particular, the development of the airport system has been exponential, with Atatürk Airport being the base of Turkish Airlines until 2019—the new Istanbul Airport having been inaugurated in the previous year. The aggressive and profitable policies of Turkish Airlines both in freight and passenger transport are assisted by the city's geographical position.

While waiting for the nation to join the European Union, and for 2009 to fulfill a dream that began eighty-five years earlier, in what Nobel Prize winner Orhan Pamuk calls "the little Turkish republic," its first capital took the title of European Capital of Culture, a nomination Turkey was working seriously toward, and for which the Istanbul Modern was inaugurated in 2004, modelled on London's Tate Modern but located on the Bosporus instead of the Thames, with a permanent collection of national artists but also hosting major international names such as Andreas Gurski and Adrian Paci, exhibitions of masters of photography promoted by agencies such as Magnum and companies such as Kodak, and the great biennials of art and design, among which the one curated in 2015 by Carolyn Christov-Bakargiev stands out, organized around a material—sea salt—that is constitutive of every history of the city, but also of everybody, antidote and enemy of a purely digital experience of life. A memorable exhibition recounted in 1500 works some 8500 years of history, from the stories of Jason and the Argonauts and the Golden Fleece, to Leon Trotsky's surreal residence on the Sea of Marmara between 1929 and 1923, the latter portrayed by an installation by one of the greatest living artists, the South African William Kentridge.

As European Capital of Culture, Istanbul was visited by world-renowned artists and designers and tourists in droves from all over the world. This was all part of an ongoing procedure to confirm the de facto Europeanism that is firmly rooted in businesses and among university students and hospitality workers. In 2009, the London School of Economics and the director of its Urban Age project, Ricky Burdett, chose Istanbul for comparative research on the new megacities of the 21st century, regarding Istanbul as the city of intersections. Deyan Sudjic, director of the Design Museum in London and author of the book *Endless*

City,[1] said in his introduction to the three-day project: "If London is the number one global city in Europe, Istanbul seems to be number two in the continent. Istanbul is the passport Turkey needs to enter Europe."

But this day has not yet come. And one can reasonably assume that it will not arrive for another quarter of a century…

Relaunch

A dual strategic plan to make life easier for citizens and attract more businesses and tourists

Since the worldwide release of Orhan Pamuk's memoir *Istanbul*, published in 2003,[2] three years before he was awarded the Nobel Prize in Literature, and before the debates arising from the international event organized in the Turkish capital by the London School of Economics, the centrality of Istanbul in the world's urban landscape was evident and well-founded. It was Saskia Sassen, one of the leading scholars in the field, who reminds us that a 2009 study by A.T. Kearney, surveying sixty cities on the planet and assessing their economic activities, human capital, information exchange, cultural vibrancy, and political engagement, placed Istanbul in the top ten in the latter category—defined as the ability to influence international political actions and political dialogue—along with Washington, Beijing, Paris, Cairo, London, and Brussels. But what seems even more important in the same research was Istanbul's ability to be a "magnet capable of attracting diverse groups of people and talent," ranking fifteenth in a panel of cities that included Tokyo, New York, Hong Kong, Chicago, Sydney, and London. In the first decade of this third millennium, thanks to the huge number of international schools in the city, Istanbul was not only attracting investment and tourists, but was also a melting pot that should be able to develop a strategic role "at the intersection of different geographies, economic and geopolitical."

A question arises: How is it possible that a city so naturally cosmo-

---

[1] Ricky Burdett and Deyan Sudjic (eds.), *Endless City. The Urban Age Project by the London School of Economics and Deutsche Bank's Alfred Herrhausen Society* (London: Phaidon, 2007).

[2] Orhan Pamuk, *İstanbul: hatiralar ve şehir* (İstanbul: YKY, 2003), translated as *Istanbul. Memories and the City* (New York: Knopf, 2005).

politan, so sharply analyzed over the centuries by great foreign writers and now finally being described by its own native narrators, so decisively oriented toward the market economy, able to host a variety of religious faiths and types of cultural offerings, has gradually fallen apart and become a space for the clash of civilizations instead of a powerful engine of peace and creativity? Is this because of the political metamorphosis of Erdoğan? He was initially a politician who presented himself as a liberal mayor capable of asserting himself thanks to the practicality of his choices rather than his ideological visions, but then turned out to be, at a time when the city of which he was the flagbearer was generating projects of global importance, the proponent of a neo-conservative movement that has even led to the redefinition of interreligious spaces that are highly emblematic for the international community, such as the Hagia Sofia.

We will find the answer in a few pages, in the inspired words of a great observer of urban realities, Richard Sennett. For now, let us content ourselves with observing the major projects and, above all, the strategies imagined by Mayor Topbaş for the decade 2014–2023, including the one that will bring the city and the entire state to the centenary celebrations of the Republic of Turkey.

After the international crisis of 2008, which only partially affected Turkey, and going back further in time to 2001, to the dramatic moment of Al Qaeda's attack on the Twin Towers, Istanbul has not only never stopped growing, but has also become an ever younger city, with an ever-increasing need for urban spaces built based on a new assumed identity: that of a more Arab and less European Turkey. The city has thus decided to have a double development plan: one for the citizens, based on infrastructure, transport, services, and also security and public order; and a second, more refined and paradoxically less discussed by local stakeholders, capable of enhancing the capital's attractiveness.

The first, defined through more than 400 workshops attended by a total of about 1000 representatives of urban interests as well as experts, opinion leaders, and employees of municipal organizations, has had a very long journey, which started in 2006, ended for the first time in 2011, then restarted and finally ended in 2013. Despite the direct commitment of the mayor, who wanted a series of internal organizational changes to the administrative machine and the control of overall objectives—it was aimed at improving performance for the inhabitants—the plan appears to have been very impersonal, almost mechanical. The first element was risk management, as if a natural disaster or terrorist attack could be at the heart of the relationship between the city and its citizens—and if one thinks of the years that followed, of the clashes between the youth and fringes of the population not aligned with the new single-mindedness of the national government, this focus does not seem so wrong. The second point relates to all large contemporary metropolises: the management of environmental values. From 2002 to 2009, Istanbul experienced an enormous infrastructural growth, with an impressive increase in the number of kilometers of railway line but no decrease in the number of privately owned vehicles caused by the affordability of cars and the growth in population with the emergence of endless satellite districts, to which it was not only costly but also difficult to extend public infrastructure. This is why the third objective, and perhaps the most interesting, was zoning. This was the least Mediterranean in terms of urban management models and the most similar to Anglo-Saxon experiences in both Europe and North America. It involved the digital and cohesive mapping of everything that was happening in individual neighborhoods, with the dual mandate of verifying in real time the concrete needs of citizens and coordinating the actions of the various parties that had to carry out the works without having to start from scratch each time when connecting to urban subservices. This innovative way of working was politically very shrewd, as it tied in seamlessly with the fourth pillar of the mayor's strategy: that of having strong control over urban space. This control was necessary so that the 'megacity' of 14 million inhabitants did not turn into a space in which everyone could do what they wanted. It was a call for order that was linked to the quality of temporary architecture and waste management in the former slums, as well as the behavior of individuals, with particular attention being paid to the presence of illegal businesses, beggars, and homeless people who could use urban interstices as a refuge.

However, there is something worrying in this apparently obvious measure, which leads one to consider the possibility of total control of all deviance, of the absence of a minimum of freedom for urban drop-outs, who are unfortunately a frequent, perhaps a natural consequence of the so-called urban century (it is important to reflect on this issue, perhaps by considering what happens every day between Sixth and Seventh Avenues in San Francisco: the height of perceived poverty in one of the places of greatest real wealth).

At the heart of the strategy was the theme of culture, which preceded that of care, of punctual attention to the socially deprived, and the great theme of transport, the most obvious from day to day. These topics were not detailed; they did not have precise actions allocated to them, but rather were frames that looked more like an administrative moral overview composed of watchwords instead of a road map that was accompanied by precise timetables and definite resources. Significant, however, is the fact that the culture theme was given the goal of internationalization, through the continuous expansion of the city's UNESCO sites, the multiplication of events that would reach an ever-larger audience, and the strengthening of a network of cities and nonlocal partners to give greater quality and consistency to the cultural product.

Much more detailed and exciting is the strategic plan of the metropolitan region around Istanbul. Launched in 2016 with a target date of 2023, it consists of three development axes, twenty-three priorities, fifty-seven strategic actions, and no fewer than 476 specific measures (perhaps rather too many!). The vision is very clear and even beautiful: "Unique Istanbul; City of Innovation and Culture with Creative and Free Citizens." Istanbul is indeed a unique city; but who could imagine it to be a sum of innovation and culture, of creativity and free citizens, and to be working towards the good of the individual and the community?

Orhan Pamuk, with considerable understatement, speaks of the age-old sadness of the city's inhabitants, who be considered, in their most active components, to be above all serious and conscientious inhabitants of a large port where there is a continuous exchange not only of goods, but also of ideas, relationships, and projects. Giving a new entrepreneurial impetus is the focus of this action by an unspecified development agency, coordinated by twelve renowned experts, who envisage a city for 2023 "in which people live and work with pleasure, and make the best use of their freedom and creativity both for their own personal improvement and for supporting society." In this public document, drafted and approved within the framework of the demands of the Ministry of Economic Development (taking full account of the fact that Istanbul includes 20 percent of the country's population and 20 percent of the GDP, and ranks fifty-fifth in the world for attractiveness but only ninetieth for qualified human capital), an inclusive society is envisioned, one that is "capable of taking on the challenges and difficulties at hand, capable of creating new urban spaces in which people of all religions, languages, races, and genders can realize their potential and pursue their dreams, inspired by the very spaces in which they live."

These statements sound appropriate for an open and inclusive world. However, the strategic plan came into being at a time that was marked by the Gezi Park protest of 2013, the clash of millions of citizens against a model of economic and political development, including the centralization of political power and the strengthening of public control in Turkey's two main cities, Ankara and Istanbul, and the associated powerful negative economic rebound. Turkey, which had been growing by 8 percent year on year until 2011, dropped to a growth rate of no more than 2.5 percent between 2012 and 2016; tourism, one of the two main pillars of this development, was immediately halted by the results of the protest (the city being put to the sword by the police to drive away the demonstrators brought about an immediate cancellation of more than 40 percent of bookings from all over the world), and was then almost wiped out by three events that hit the international news: the terrorist acts suffered by Istanbul in 2016 and 2017, the former claimed by the Kurds and the latter by Isis, and the attempted coup in July 2016.

Stabilization

From the Europe of religions to politics as religion

This is a time when Istanbul's history of development, its destiny as the recognized capital of the Mediterranean at the center of the large Euro-Asian region—a hub of knowledge and quality production, a tourist attraction to which new infrastructures and new professions are linked—risks a setback, and requires strong initiatives for its relaunch. It was the deputy interior minister himself who declared during the Gezi Park protest that it was a Western plot to ensure that Istanbul would not have a bigger and more influential airport than Frankfurt—at which point tempers frayed even further, positions became entrenched, and the ideological clash became destructive.

It is no coincidence that the regional development plan proposes to work toward a physical environment that not only meets the needs of citizens, but is also endowed with quality, impeccable design, and rich authenticity. This last word is one of the key terms of the contemporary urban debate—and of the exceptional role of Istanbul.

After hosting the 2010 European Capital of Culture as a nonmember state but waiting to be admitted and hoping to become a central stabilizing factor in the stability of the new Europe, Turkey (in particular Istanbul but also Izmir) has been trying to host even bigger and more important events, capable of both affirming the greatness and importance of the state and activating direct resources for powerful and possibly unscrupulous redevelopment. Smyrna challenged Milan for the 2015 Expo, Istanbul, Tokyo, and Madrid for the 2020 Olympics—a contest won by Tokyo. Expressing much intellectual honesty, the regional plan specifies that "the rapid economic growth of a nation does not necessarily make it a place of equitable development. In many economically developed nations, social problems cannot be solved without establishing a relationship between economic growth and the quality of human resources."

Based on the *Human Development Report*, from which the data given here on economic development and human resources have been taken, the document expresses the hope that in 2023 Istanbul will truly be at the center of East and West, a place where relations with the rest of the world are able to grow incrementally, and the other urban economic functions are embedded in an international value chain that is determined by competitiveness into which the city's creative and innovative workforce can be integrated. At the same time, there are clear problems in the relationships between the center and the suburbs. It is strongly argued that the latter will be developed with their own centers of attraction, integrating welfare services and spaces for cultural activities, social initiatives, and research activities together with artistic events. In its general outline, it would be very useful to propose and apply this plan both to other large international metropolises (such as the segregated Sao Paulo in Brazil and the boundless Mexico City) and to European and Italian cities (how can we not think of Turin, Rome, and also Genoa and Venice?).

There is no space here to elaborate further on a 200-page document that explains with text, diagrams, and high-quality pictures how Istanbul should position itself, what weight to give to its new entrepreneurship, and how to maintain authenticity when there is a chance to stabilize development. In the text, the concepts of collaboration and good governance recur, as well as the importance of feeling proud of being born and/or being resident in a place that has decided to focus on the "learning society" and yet invites its citizens to reflect on traditions to carry them strongly and courageously into the future, preserving the values and consciousness of its civilization.

These concepts seem to be at the basis of a new model of city and state in which localism, of which we boast, is the basis for a new globalism. As the great philosopher Bernard Stiegler said, this is one of the great questions of our time: how to maintain the quality of the feeling of a territory, without it becoming a separatist obsession. This question, which we encountered in our trip to Barcelona a few chapters ago, returns even more powerfully in Istanbul. Richard Sennett can help us to deepen the concept, to treat it with less superficiality, perhaps realizing that we can use the same words to define different situations. In his prepapers for the meetings held in Istanbul with the London School of Economics team, he recalls:

> It has often been said that a new generation of cities has emerged in Europe, whose links are often closer between them than between these cities and the states to which they belong. This statement is both true and false. The image of a "Europe of cities" concerns the networks between these centers, not the cities as a whole. Population movements from one suburb to another are very rare indeed: a few Turkish families pushed to the fringes of Frankfurt are ready to make a spontaneous migration to the fringes of London, and there is very little movement between the suburbs of London and those of Paris.

This is the concept that development workers are confronted with. I would add that the power of contemporary communication, linked to that of finance, causes an effect that is perhaps trivial but worth clarifying. The mythologies of cities are linked to a brand that always looks at the best of what they can offer. Even if there are fans of urban margins, who refer to their "truth" and to their "realism," the urban reality that we choose as a place where our children will study, that we move to for work, where we start a new company, or simply spend a period as temporary citizens, never focuses on the dystopian element, but rather on something that positively attracts us. This attraction is all the stronger when, upon personally visiting the place, we recognize its originality mixed with standardization. Unlike the nineteenth-century French narrators mentioned (and loved, evidently) by Pamuk, we not only look for differences in our urban travels and passions, but also for similarities, which reassure us. Moreover, the demand for safety is so great that it involves not only numerical but also visual standards. The ability to cope with risk appears to be more and more similar to our relationship with suffering, not to say death: Although these are integral parts of the life cycle, we definitely want to exclude them from our daily path.

This imagery, by virtue of global communication and in particular social media, now involves everyone in what can be described as a profoundly horizontal way (in Italy, a brilliant and acute writer such as Francesco Piccolo has realized this). Everyone is therefore asking to live in or visit places that are easily explored, and the most visited cities are increasingly those that offer all their beauty in a long walk, a tour that doesn't involve forced stops or entrance fees to museums. These cities are built as spaces for visiting—visiting that blends with living.

However, as Sennett reminds us, "the resurgence of cultural nationalism signals in part the refusal of people outside the center to be aligned, to have taken their invisibility for granted, to regard the 'local' as semi-decent. The center/periphery distinction generates profound dissonances, and this is a major problem that cities like Istanbul face when they begin a period of strong expansion."

Paradoxically, not only does setting concrete goals sometimes cause bigger problems to be solved than those that were initially considered, but also destructive elements are brought into play by growth, requiring attention to be paid to the balance between masses and power: This is not easy to acquire and often not even desired.

Thus, the bourgeois liberalism of Erdoğan's early days as mayor, his practical tackling of problems, his praising of the city and its inhabitants as the sole referents of his actions (first bypassing city councils and then, once he became prime minister and then president, demanding direct representation linked to the power of the people and not intermediated by anyone who was democratically elected), became a demand for the form and observance of rules of just one part (it does not matter which part) of the population, and not of the whole. Thus, causing the greatest of distortions, as Sennett writes at the end of his speech for Istanbul: "If there is a danger that we as policy makers, planners and architects must face, it is how we can protect and promote informal public spaces. Both challenges, that of centralization and non-formalization, pose a question: Will Istanbul in the future be like the modern Frankfurt or the Venice of the Renaissance?"

Future

The return of a new Atatürk

From April 2014 to April 2019, Ekrem İmamoğlu was mayor of a western quarter of Istanbul called Beylikdüzü; a quarter where everyone loved him for the calmness with which he listened to them and the concrete way in which he realized their demands, framing them in a broader scheme. Not surprisingly, it was they, the immigrant inhabitants from the rest of Turkey, who told the other 12.5 million Stambuliotes that İmamoğlu was the best mayor they could wish for. A quarter of a century after Erdoğan's appointment to the Topkapı, after two rounds in which the president himself tried to disavow İmamoğlu and reduce his powers by, for instance, placing some of the city's most important historical assets in the hands of the Ministry of Culture in Ankara (among others, the Galata Tower, the keys to which were handed over by the Genoese to Muhammad II the Conqueror in 1453), İmamoğlu is using the same method with all his fellow citizens. He is an immigrant himself, born in 1970 in Trazbon (the famous Trebizond, a city of sailors on the shores of the Black Sea) and arrived in Istanbul in the late 1980s for study. His master's degree in human resources management corresponds perfectly to the challenge of the moment: Once the city is done, it is time to be a citizen. It is no longer necessary to make Istanbul grow. More competent human resources are needed, as the regional development plan states. Peace and sharing are required as the basis for a new prosperity. This is a strongly secular city, which looks with suspicion at the transformation of Hagia Sofia into a mosque and with great concern at investments in the war industry instead of a boost in energy sustainability. İmamoğlu knows, however, that he does not have to choose sides. In a city that is all about competitions, with four football and three basketball teams, at least three religions, and two internal currents within one of them (headed by related economic interests), the young people and families who protested in Gezi Park seven years ago are demanding more tolerance and new opportunities for development.

As in Wrocław, as in London, as in Hong Kong, the contest is between these diffuse urban elites—who are not always economically rich, but are certainly collectively well educated—and the rest of the country, a 75 percent population that must figure out whether and how to trust its new sultan. A sultan who is still relatively young, in force, but dedicated to settling, as is always the case, accusations of isolationism with small and large wars, most recently the one with Cyprus. İmamoğlu has been fifteen years in power, has a secular conservative party behind him, and has a big city to revive after a five-year slump. Perhaps for this reason Erdoğan tried in every way to remove him from office, with the complicity of the Istanbul Court, which on March 23, 2025, imprisoned İmamoğlu on charges of corruption and abuse of power.

Istanbul and the whole of Turkey have for months been in a state of intense popular mobilization: the protests—the largest of the past decade along with those of Gezi Park in 2013—continue to fill Sarachane Square in Istanbul and the streets of other major cities such as Ankara and Izmir, despite harsh police repression, which has already led to about 700 arrests and an extension of the ban on public gatherings.

Meanwhile, the main opposition party, the CHP, has officially designated İmamoğlu as its candidate to challenge Erdoğan in the next presidential elections. The political crisis strikes a country already in deep difficulty, and for years now, not least because of Erdoğan's unorthodox economic policies: the Turkish lira has lost more than 40 percent of its value in the past year, inflation exceeds 75 percent, and Turkey has fallen to 117th place out of 142 countries in the World Justice Project's global rule of law index.

İmamoğlu is considered the main political rival of President Erdoğan ahead of the 2028 presidential elections. Twice elected mayor of Istanbul, he has defeated candidates backed by the ruling AKP party and is now seen as the only figure truly capable of challenging the president's grip on power. For this reason, according to the opposition and many analysts, the legal proceedings against him are nothing more than a tool to eliminate him from the political arena. The charges he faces are often vague, based on flimsy evidence or forced interpretations, in a context where, according to international organizations, Turkey's judiciary has lost its independence. "The goal is to prevent him from running," CHP leaders declare. A final conviction, even in just one of the open trials, could bar him from public office, rendering him ineligible.

"With the most popular rival of President Recep Tayyip Erdoğan now in prison, the arrest of hundreds of others in investigations against the Republican People's Party (CHP), and rumors circulating that the government may seek to even take over the party, Turkey is on the cusp of a transition to a consolidated dictatorship," said Nate Schenkkan, former research director at Freedom House.[3]

Will the cities prevail, or will the states once again block the democratic process that grows from the grassroots, from the territories? This, too, is part of the urban paradox.

---

[3] Nate Schenkkan, *The End of Competitive Authoritarianism in Turkey* (Freedom House, 2025).

7 Wrocław
A city for young people

A buffer city

A city built on twelve islands, connected by more than a hundred bridges, one in which four languages are habitually spoken: This is not Amsterdam, nor is it Venice; but compared with the former it has a greater rate of innovation, and compared with the latter has enough young residents to make the most important African or Asian metropolises envious. It is Wrocław, or Breslau, the third most populous city in Poland, which has a unique story that involves resilience, destruction, and the ability to plan, one that has been written thanks in part to the coordination of an innovative mayor, Rafal Dutkiewicz, who has several times been nominated as the best mayor in the world.

Wrocław is a border city, but above all a connecting city. Very close to Germany, and therefore easily occupied both during Prussian hegemony and of course during Nazism, it was inhabited by Germans who replaced the Polish population that was almost exterminated during World War Two. In 1945, there were about 190,000 German inhabitants and 17,000 Poles. Between 1945 and 1949, the former were almost all driven out of the city, and those who decided to stay later had to tell a specially constituted tribunal how they had behaved before and during the war. In 1946, there were fewer than 200,000 inhabitants. The deportations and battles, in particular the Russian siege of a city that had been devastated by five years of fighting, not only completely destroyed the Jewish component, so lively and flourishing before 1938, but also torn apart the Slavic and German components. Over 18,000 people died of the cold in January 1945, and by the time German co-commander Karl Hanke raised the white flag on May 6, shortly before the official end of the war, over 40,000 dead lay in the colorful baroque houses that are now visited by over 5 million tourists a year. At the end of the massacres, the Poles, who had largely fled to Lviv, returned to live in the city while the future of Poland, once again a buffer state between Germany and Russia—as had already happened between Russia and Prussia in 1797—was debated worldwide.

Crisis

For more than thirty years, this history has weighed heavily on the relations between states and between cities located on either side of the border—a blurred border that has no significant mountains or rivers to mark it. It is only since the fall of the Berlin Wall, forty years after the events briefly described in the previous section, that Wrocław, a city twice emptied and twice rebuilt not only physically but also and above all culturally, fifty years after those events, decided to take its destiny into its own hands and to completely rethink it.

Rafal Dutkiewicz, born in 1959 in Mikstat, a suburb of Wrocław, graduated from the Technical University of Wrocław in applied mathematics in 1982 and was awarded a PhD in mathematical logic from the Catholic University of Lublin in 1986. These were his formative years, with frequent trips to Germany, where he studied for a PhD at the University of Freiburg, which above all brought his first political engagement. In his early twenties he joined the trade union Solidarność (Solidarity), becoming first its secretary then president for the city of Wrocław. The 1990s saw him involved in the transition of post-socialist Poland, which soon became a buffer between reunified Germany, the development of the new public kingdoms of Czechia and Slovakia, and the ever-strong political interests of Mother Russia. The population of Wrocław became predominantly Polish again, but the unemployment rate was very high, and people's level of education very low, especially among women.

Dutkiewicz became mayor of the city in 2002, a year before the referendum for Poland's entry into the European Union, of which he was a great promoter. Urban unemployment stood at 13 percent, rural unemployment at 18 percent. Female unemployment was also at 18 percent. But ten years later it was reduced to 5 percent, but only in the metropolitan area. Rural unemployment has yet to fall below 12.5 percent.

Relaunch

The university town

Dutkiewicz's own background immediately encouraged him to make knowledge the central asset for Wrocław's development. The investment, agreed with Warsaw, was huge: 250 million euro. In just a few years, the city's university's focus on the local system changed to a true internationalization of curricula, in step with the demands of an evolving world of work.

In the first phase, the market this offer looked to was naturally the local one: Lower Silesia, Poland. But quickly higher education became Wrocław's key asset: a great dream that rapidly transformed the whole of Poland, taking it from 400,000 students in the 1990/1991 school year, the first after the fall of the Wall, to almost 2 million in 2018. Today, with ten public and three private universities, and with over 150,000 students from all over the world but especially from the rest of Europe, Wrocław is truly a university city.

As is often the case in Eastern European cities, especially those with a strong Prussian tradition, technical universities have always played an important role in Wrocław. Out of a total of thirteen, the three polytechnic universities are the most attractive for students who wish to explore research. However, the secret of Wrocław's attractiveness lies in its very low cost: for accommodation, you do not have to spend more than 300 euro per month; to eat and have fun, you do not need a big budget. The city also boasts student-friendly organizations, and every weekend offers a wide range of sports, cultural, and food and wine activities.

Students are therefore not simply attracted but positively welcomed and well cared for. From the moment they enroll, they have a companion (a "buddy") who picks them up when they arrive in the city and helps them to settle in. The entry into the "Erasmus machine" represents a true moment of transition for them. For about a million young Europeans, Wrocław has been a triple threshold over the past ten years, marking a transition from the world of study to the world of work; from a restricted to an enlarged community; from a universe of potential to that of responsibility. In this sense, Wrocław is a very encouraging location for students from dozens of different nationalities.

The mayor's idea to enhance human capital by attracting talent was complemented by his other excellent work: that of attracting large and medium-sized enterprises, which, using European funds, moved not their production sites, but their research, technology transfer, and service centers to Wrocław.

The city of innovation

The dedicated effort of the mayor and all his collaborators to make Wrocław an international university city were connected to a second major goal: to completely overhaul the labor market, taking advantage of a significant population growth that, contrary to the OECD's assumption in 2013, has not proved to be a bubble but rather an engine of change. Combined with the arrival of more than a million students from the rest of the world in about fifteen years, this enabled the city to attract centers of expertise for major international brands.

In just three years, from 2008 to 2010, the city doubled the number of jobs available in the business sector: from 5,000 to 10,000. But even more significant was the growth in university degrees between 2011 and 2020: 26 to 70 percent of citizens can now boast a university degree.

Thanks to a "door-to-door" promotion that he directly took charge of, with an impressive number of foreign missions to the main innovation centers worldwide, the mayor brought to Wrocław such economic players as Bosch, McKinsey & Company, Nokia, Siemens, and Volvo, as well as dozens of smaller brands that chose the city because of its central location in the new twenty-seven-member Europe, the possibility of tax breaks, the low cost of intellectual labor, and the large number of talented young people, willing to do internships and interested in a first entry into the world of work.

At the heart of all these initiatives was the European Institute of Technology, founded in 2007, which had two focuses. The first was on nanotechnology applied to materials and the second was dedicated to biotechnology, which had important links to the biomedical sector. Thanks to these programs, the city has been able to combine a strongly horizontal policy (bringing as many young people as possible to study in a "frontier" location) with a vertical policy, specializing in sectors with high added value, capable of satisfying the needs of existing companies (e.g. the white goods sector for industrial or domestic use) or companies that wanted to expand in strongly emerging sectors such as the life sciences, undoubtedly one of the fastest growing in the ten-year perspective.

The mayor's individual experience became a model for his city. A researcher himself, a student abroad, and a profound connoisseur of the needs of small and medium-sized enterprises in particular, for example those that cannot afford to have their own research center or to independently attract and grow a team of talents on their own, Dutkiewicz gradually succeeded in creating an appropriate urban ecosystem through the building of ad hoc departments within the municipal machine.

An example of this was his facility in making Wrocław one of McKinsey & Company's six global knowledge hubs. The McKinsey Knowledge Centre in Wrocław is part of a network that also has an office in Waltham (Massachusetts), two in India, one in China, and one in Costa Rica; it is the fast-growing European hub of one of the world's largest consulting firms. Within it, hundreds of employees interact in the service of network projects. This is an excellent example of the positioning that the city has built with dedication over more than a decade.

Stabilization

The city of culture

Unlike Matera's experience, which we investigate in Chapter 8, Wrocław's candidacy as European Capital of Culture in 2016 was not the starting point, but the culmination of a decade-long process of change. Beating even Warsaw in the first competition between Polish cities to boast this title, Wrocław demonstrated a considerable degree of participatory planning, capable of combining medium- to long-term visions and concrete implementation skills.

The city has staked a great deal on its DNA as a center of research and development, with no fewer than nine of its citizens being awarded the Nobel Prize in the little over one hundred years of the prize's existence (almost one every ten years, a record),[1] and has stressed this asset as a company would have done, or perhaps a better comparison is a sports team, in order to achieve the coveted title of European Capital of Culture.

---

1 See, for instance, https://visitwroclaw.eu/en/nobel-prize-winners-from-wroclaw, October 18, 2016.

An example is that of Jerzy Grotowski. Born in Rzersow, a tiny village in south-eastern Poland in 1933, he moved to Wrocław in 1965. The playwright and theater director realized that in a city still immersed in the communist tradition, an idea of "poor theater" that completely re-thought contemporary theater, giving stage art a new role of reflection in both the social and religious context. Grotowski's teaching gave rise to the theater of contemporary masters such as Eugenio Barba and Peter Brook, but also provided a profound lesson for his fellow citizens, who over the course of time paid him more and more attention, to the point of dedicating a theater research center to him.

This starting point, linked to the dramatic history of Wrocław, a city that has been destroyed and rebuilt several times, is certainly one of the great themes that helped the city win the title of Capital of Culture, the seal on the long and conscious work of rethinking and repositioning that was carried out by the mayor over fifteen years.

The major events around European Capital of Culture 2016 were a huge success for Wrocław. Over the course of the year, the city hosted around two thousand cultural events, with 170,000 people actively involved in the various projects and more than 5 million attendees.

At the opening press conference, Mayor Rafał Dutkiewicz rightly emphasized that the European Capital of Culture project was the most important in Wrocław's postwar history. Although Wrocław had always chosen to devote a large amount of space to culture (it is estimated that it invests 50 million euro in it every year), the effort in 2016 was certainly exceptional. In that year, around 100 million euro was spent on the cultural program alone, which put the city at the center of attention, and another 300 million euro was added for the creation of new permanent cultural infrastructure. The city was thus enriched with new and important cultural spaces: the Pavilion of the Four Domes (the new home of the Museum of Contemporary Art), the National Music Forum, the Pan Tadeusz Museum, the Centrum Historii Zajezdnia, the Capitol Theater, the Fama Library and Cultural Centre, the Formaty Club, and the "Barbara" Infopoint, entirely dedicated to culture.

But the most intelligent choices made Wrocław the meeting point of many new talents, real cultural startups, connected to the more general system of innovation and the fundamental topic of creative industries.

The inauguration ceremony

An example of this repositioning was the opening ceremony celebrating Wrocław's inauguration as European Capital of Culture, which was held on Sunday January 17, 2016. The main event was directed by Chris Baldwin and was called Przebudzenie, meaning Awakening. The production involved a huge number of citizens, divided into four processions from different parts of Wrocław, all of which reached the central Market Square. Each of the processions was symbolically led by one of the four Spirits of Wrocław (Pluralism, Innovation, Reconstruction, and Flood), each representing a different aspect of the city's history. The spectacle was impressive, with the participation of around 1400 costumed people, 300 cyclists, 200 choristers, and 50 soldiers. As many as thirty illuminated signs and thirty huge puppets were used to enhance the choreography.

Baldwin made it clear that his aim was to reconstruct the city's cultural journey, imagining it as a moment of coming together not only of contemporary citizens, who have been able to overcome the fragmentation of the contemporary and feel part of one big community again, but also to represent the reunion of five different peoples—Polish, Czech, German, Ukrainian, and Jewish—who have played a role in the various stages of the city's history and now finally live together peacefully in Wrocław and Europe.

A decisive role was played by the various citizens' cultural associations, who reconnected the numerous bridges with which the city is dotted, which historically united it as a group of islands: Each bridge was dedicated to an individual display, and citizens who crossed them emphasized these themes, which were both symbolic and concrete, with voices and lights.

The ceremony on January 17 was preceded by two days of events. On Friday January 15, an exhibition by Basque sculptor Eduardo Chillida was presented at the Awangarda BWA Gallery. On Saturday, January 16, an exhibition of the finalists from the last twenty-five editions of the Mies van der Rohe Award, a contemporary architecture prize organized by the EU, was opened. On the same day, the National Museum was transformed into the Muzeum Marześ (Museum of Dreams), where nine performances, directed by Jacqueline Kornmüller, were staged, combining literary, theatrical, and musical works about dreams and fantasy. The weekend was also marked by some hundred events, including a series of concerts at the Narodowe Forum Muzyki (the National Music Forum) and various performances in the city's main public spaces, including stations, shopping centers, and hospitals.

The Capital of Culture year as a strengthening of the national and international network

Numerous projects were launched in 2016 that had long-lasting effects, such as those concerning the redevelopment of courtyards and green parks, the creation of a new House of Culture, and the overall sustainability of the event.

Most of the projects saw the active contribution of the citizens, who were able to undertake specific initiatives as an integral part of the program. As many as fifty-two ideas were realized of the original 464 proposals. Among those that materialized thanks to the participation of the inhabitants of Wrocław were the decorating of lampposts and benches, meetings in parks with readings, sports performances, and children's games.

Particularly significant in the context of the Wrocław Open City project was cooperation with the Ukrainian city of Lviv, from which during the 20th century so many families arrived; they still live in the city today. During April, Ukraine was the host country for an event that featured dozens of events, providing the opportunity to listen to traditional music and songs, taste regional dishes, and learn about Ukrainian traditions.

Similarly, opportunities were organized to learn about other Polish cities: Gdańsk, Katowice, Łódź, Lublin, Poznań, and Szczecin.

Musical events that will remain in the hearts of citizens and tourists alike included concerts by the great Ennio Morricone, David Gilmour, and the Rammstein Band; International Jazz Day; the performance of the opera *Zarzuela* at the Municipal Stadium; and Singing Europe. The Thanks Jimi Festival gave the city another Guinness World Record, thanks to the many guitarists who came to the Rynek (the city market square, one of the largest in Poland).

Among the other spectacles were the European Film Awards ceremony, the initiatives organized for the European Night of Literature, and the fireworks that accompanied celebrations relating to the city's appointment as World Book Capital, which we will talk about in a moment.

Art took center stage with, among other things, the previously mentioned exhibition of sculptures by Eduardo Chillida and another at the Museum of Architecture of the works of local architect Jadwiga Grabowska Hawrylak, as well as the exhibition "A Way to Modernity. The Werkbund Estates 1927–1932." The opening of the Four Domes Pavilion during the year gave the city new exhibition spaces for contemporary art, enabling the hosting of various initiatives, including "The Wrocław Europe," "Summer Rental," and "Photography Never Dies."

The legacy of Grotowsky and "poor theater" gave a special role to theater productions. In 2016, Wrocław hosted the Theater Olympiad, becoming the most significant venue for viewing and reflecting on this ever-renewing art. New performances by some of the most famous contemporary playwrights were staged: Eugenio Barba, Romeo Castellucci, Pippo Delbono, Peter Brook, Jan Fabre, Walerij Fokin, Heiner Hoebbels, Krystian Lupa, Tadashi Suzuki, Theodoros Terzopoulos, and Robert Wilson.

The closing ceremony was particularly moving, leaving the citizens with the realization that the event, which had been significant for the city and in some respects was a historic moment, would be a truly important future asset. It was no coincidence that the city choir, the star of the ceremony, chanted the phrase "The European Capital of Culture is within us."

World Book Capital

In 2016, Wrocław was not only the European Capital of Culture, but also the World Book Capital, a coveted award given annually by UNESCO to the city that is most committed to the promotion and dissemination of reading as a tool for knowledge and development. This was the first time a Polish city had been appointed, and also the first time that the two events had taken place at the same venue in the same year.

The program of events was extensive and interesting. Among many, we would like to mention the customary Wrocławskie Targi Dobrych Książek, the Fair of Good Books, held in the renovated premises of the Central Railway Station, and the Cycle of Self-Descriptions for Theater Performances, which takes place in the city every year.

The run-up to 2016 also saw Wrocław host prestigious literary events. The European Night of Literature in 2014 should be mentioned. During this event, ten texts by European authors were performed, each at a different and impressive site in the historical center, including the old prison courtyard in Więzienna Street, the garden of the Royal Palace, the WRO Art Centre, Kino Nowe Horyzonty, and the former Faculty of Pharmacy and Medicine in Grodzka Street. It was a veritable literary marathon during which, from 6 p.m. to 11 p.m., every half hour, excerpts from unpublished books were read.

A key role was again played by children, who were the true protagonists of the event, particularly of the Children and Young Adults Literature Festival—a meeting place for passionate under-eighteen-year-old readers.

The city of tourism

One of Wrocław's stated goals when the city decided to enter the competition for European Capital of Culture in 2008 was to double the number of tourists from 2 million to 4 million per year. This was achieved, and indeed surpassed: The events organized in 2016 led to around 5 million overnight stays and truly exceptional appreciation levels, which the city was able to repeat in the following years. In 2018, it became European Best Destination, ahead of Bilbao, Colmar, Hvar, Riga, and Milan, thanks to 41,000 votes from over 146 different nations. It is no coincidence that Mayor Dutkiewicz, at the end of his third and final term of office before handing over to a new young mayor—aged forty, as he himself had been at the beginning of this great story of urban, economic, social, and cultural renewal—was able to declare himself extraordinarily satisfied with the result. Having attracted young talents with a policy of expanding the university offer based on a solid tradition, and also with a unique opportunity to spend European funds; having transformed an area used to being autonomous and self-referential into the heart of a network of innovation and research; having attracted over forty international companies; and having made Wrocław an award-winning tourist destination on a par with Porto, Bordeaux, Lisbon, and Copenhagen, the mayor can indeed say that he has brought the great urban repositioning action he promoted to a climax. The objective of the European Best Destination website, managed by Brussels, is to promote tourism in Europe by selecting the most attractive destinations. Cities compete by asking for votes, especially from travel agencies and tourism experts working in the media. This is not an end in itself, but part of an investment aimed at producing lasting results. It can only be achieved if an up-to-date database of all opinion leaders in the sector is built up and a process is set in motion with the objective not simply to be perceived as an interesting city for one particular year, but to be a city that has made tourism—and cultural tourism in particular—a stable driving force.

Future

The clash between town and country

In fifteen years of continuous activity and renewal, Wrocław has been able to make use of every kind of resource that has been made available. Since Poland's accession to the EU, it has chosen to launch a new urban policy every two or three years without abandoning the previous ones, but rather by progressively integrating ideas and projects. Recovery of unused urban spaces, revitalization of the transport and reception infrastructure, expansion of the airport, dialogue with large foreign investment companies for the construction of new office space, redevelopment of university residences, competitions for start-ups, creation of a research focus: All the tools that an urban area can bring into play have been put to good use, making the Polish city a model for Europe and the world.

Wrocław is above all an example of how soft power can count, with a mayor who chose to build very precise alliances in constantly developing sectors, which more often took him to China, Korea, and Japan than to Brussels.

But Wrocław's challenge did not end in 2016, and the city is now facing a new level of competition that poses a new challenge to cities not only in Europe but worldwide. Can cities grow on their own, draining young people from rural areas, leaving those regions without skills and identity? Or can the development of a territory be imagined not only in favor of increasingly innovative urban centers, but also with an eye to the countryside that surrounds those centers?

The Polish political case is an example that can easily be linked with what has happened in the United States and Great Britain, and also what is perhaps determining the success of Putin in Russia and Erdoğan in Turkey. Without paying attention to rural areas, cities can no longer continue to grow in the same way. Poland's conservative vote in the July 2020 presidential elections suggests a very clear reading of this phenomenon: To give substance to the vote, the Polish progressive front even coopted the mayor of Warsaw, making the division between urban and rural areas truly visible.

This is the new challenge for cities, and for Wrocław in particular. To grow, it is not enough to network elsewhere; it is necessary to seek cooperation with neighboring areas, starting with those from which it has drained skills without giving back vision and perspective. Just as Istanbul could and should have become a fully European capital, Wrocław cannot imagine itself as anything other than serving a European federation of highly integrated states.

But this opportunity has been heavily threatened by the ongoing shifts in the international context. Poland, after coming close to becoming a second Hungary and drifting once more into the sphere of influence of Putin's Russia, returned to the polls and, with the reelection of President Tusk in December 2023, reaffirmed the need to support Ukraine but, above all, to embrace a federal Europe. Things could have gone differently, but what happened has instead strengthened Wroclaw's role in urban leadership. The young mayor Jacek Zbigniew Sutryk, first elected in 2018 in close continuity with the previous urban leader Rafał Dutkiewicz, is today president of the association of all Polish cities, and his background as a sociologist—an expert in social integration with a strong focus on individual freedoms and participation—makes him a symbol of a young socialist Poland.

Wroclaw's growth has not stopped; its population continues to increase, also because it has become one of the preferred places of refuge for Ukrainian families devastated by more than 40 months of war. Yet, despite having over 20 percent of residents under the age of 25, the overall economic situation is becoming more delicate. In recent weeks, news broke that Donald Trump's sanctions are also hitting research centers in Eastern Europe, and that Intel has decided to leave Wroclaw and refocus its innovation efforts in the United States.

By contrast, the city is deepening its quality-of-life policies, focusing not only on environmental sustainability but also on the quality of food. By joining the Delice Network—the most significant forum and project space linking food-service professionals with local urban development, founded in Lyon—Wroclaw is forging a close relationship between food policy and the future of its citizens. A project that may also have taken inspiration from the Milan Charter, signed by many governments during Expo 2015, though one that took root less in Italy (where only Turin and Reggio Emilia, along with Milan itself, developed precise cross-cutting policies based on food quality, starting with school meals) than in the rest of Europe.

Beyond environmental and social cohesion policies, Wroclaw is now at the forefront of building new relationships with the Asian economic world, particularly with China and Singapore. Attentive to the most significant international trends, and committed through specific policies to enabling its younger citizens to travel around the world with formal agreements with other cities, Wroclaw strikes a perfect balance between the values of European democratic tradition and the idea that the future of the planet lies not so much in the prerogatives of individual states, but in a platform of relationships among urban areas, business, and culture. A clear vision to be promoted—making this Polish city a truly unique example in today's global context.

8 Matera
From shame to pride

A millennial city

Christ stopped at Eboli; or, rather, in Matera. This 1000-year-old city has a history that seems to revolve around a chapter in a single book by an exiled Turinese, a physician, painter, and writer called Carlo Levi who traced in many of his pages the trajectory of the end of the first half of the twentieth century, leaving a glimpse of the legacy we could take with us. Without Levi, Matera would not have Olivetti and Pasolini, and perhaps not even Mel Gibson.

Crisis

However, it is not the crisis that some mayors of Matera faced in the 1990s that Levi tells us about in his masterpiece. Between the end of the last millennium and the beginning of the one in which we are now living, the city emerged from the shadows of the postwar period, with its economic reinvention linked to the industrial production of furniture. On the border between Puglia and Basilicata, in the Murgia Valley, tens of thousands of pieces a year were produced, capable of entering the American and Asian markets and converting craftsmanship into pocket-sized multinational designs. The 2008 financial crisis, which drew a line between the urban policies enacted until 2000 and the current ones, hit hard the producers of goods such as these, especially in this part of the South, which had not yet seen any significant growth in the cultural and tourism sector, despite the admirable example of neighboring Apulia, which was led by Nichi Vendola and a very competent and cohesive leadership team.

In 2009, on the threshold of elections, a group of young Matera residents, some still living in the city and some expatriates, read that Italy in 2019 would again (after Florence in 1985, Bologna in 2000, and Genoa in 2004) host the European Capital of Culture. This seemed a good idea for the whole community to pursue. But how to make it happen?

Relaunch

The chessboard

Competing to become the European Capital of Culture means participating in a game that has precise rules. There are two primary guidelines: the need to build a program with a strong European dimension and the opportunity to involve the citizens of the candidate city as fully as possible.

These recent rules have been made as the project has evolved; it is now one of the best known in Europe, together with the to some extent complementary Erasmus Program. The project was born in 1985 at the behest of Melina Mercouri, Greece's minister of culture, an extraordinary actress and memorable protagonist of the film *The Third Man*, directed by Carol Reed and with a screenplay by Graham Greene. She was a passionate socialist, a convinced advocate of a united Europe that would be based on culture, on the identity of peoples and their ability to listen to each other, who nourished their daily lives thanks to their respective historical roots, architectural heritage, and popular traditions.

Players

Who can take part in this game? In 1985, it was decided that one nation would be nominated each year and that a city within that nation would be selected to represent the whole of Europe. The first was, of course, Athens, the second Florence. This continued until 2000, the year in which—to celebrate the dawning millennium—it was decided to have as many as fifteen capitals, one for each of the EU member states, and to identify them on the basis of a very specific characteristic: to have been the seat of the first university in their country. In Italy, it was therefore

Bologna's turn. From 2004, with the enlargement of the EU, it was decided that there would be two capitals per year. The first two were to represent France and Italy, and Lille and Genoa were chosen, two industrial cities in search of a new role and identity. As early as 2010, it was made known that Italy would have another turn in 2019. But it was not until 2012 that a specific call was launched for potential locations, with the ad hoc focus for efforts being the Ministry of Cultural Heritage and Activities. Based on experiences in other cities and nations, it was decided that the candidacy would involve written and oral presentations, the second including an on-site visit by the judging committee, which had thirteen participants—seven international members nominated by the European Commission and six national members chosen by the ministry. It was assumed that the possibility of becoming Capital of Culture would be appealing to many, but no one thought that Italy would have even more applications than Spain in 2016 (San Sebastian was the winner from a pool of sixteen candidates). In the first selection phase of September 2013, twenty-one Italian cities were nominated; it was not known how many would be selected by the jury, as the number was not predetermined.

Tactics

Matera immediately decided to go on the offensive—to use its bid as the basis for a larger project. Based on a preliminary idea from a group of young people who had formed an association, the relevant institutions, namely the municipality, province, and region, with help from the very beginning from the Chamber of Commerce, the University of Basilicata, and even the municipality and province of Potenza, tried to create a plan that would exploit both local talents and national and international experts. Many who had dedicated themselves to similar projects were called in: the director of the Entertainment Sector of the Culture Department of the City of Milan, the Lucanian-born Antonio Calbi; one of the partners of the Fitzcarraldo Foundation, Alessandro Bollo, who had already written on the subject; an Italian professor long resident in Great Britain, Franco Bianchini, who he had assisted with then analyzed in detail Liverpool's bid for European Capital of Culture in 2008. Also involved was the current author, Paolo Verri, former director of Turin's Strategic Plan, of the celebrations for the 150th anniversary of the Unification of Italy, and before that director of the Book Fair, the driving force behind many initiatives in the Savoy city and editor of a text devoted to the relationship between major events and urban development,[1] in which the theme of Capitals of Culture is explored. Right from the start, thanks to the intelligence of Rossella Tarantino, who coordinated the candidacy process at a local level on behalf of the region and later the municipality of Matera, the city tried to stand out for its willingness to innovate: Rather than relying on local excellence or on heritage, it explored a new form of local governance that would appeal to talent as well as to businesses and tourists, systematizing an effort that had in the immediately preceding years spawned organizations such as APT Basilicata (working to attract tourists and tourism operators), Sviluppo Basilicata, Basilicata Innovazione, and the Lucana Film Commission. The region created a multifaceted, multidisciplinary task force that involved many capable, open-minded individuals who were ready to take up the challenges ahead. From the winter of 2010, every possible opportunity was taken to bring to Matera someone or something that did not yet have a relationship with the region.

The eliminations

It was not just a matter of nominating the city in order to win a title, but of searching for a basic vision that would bring alive an extraordinary heritage—one that had led to its nomination in 1993 as a UNESCO World Heritage Site. This search took place not in the confines of an office, but in many open meetings, in which above all the local creative class participated. At the heart of the new challenge was the Visioni urbane project, promoted by the Basilicata region and coordinated by Rossella Tarantino. The purpose of this initiative was to focus on young cultural operators in the area, who were called upon to stimulate through their daily activities five centers of creativity that were spread throughout the region, among which Casa Cava in the heart of the Sasso Barisano in Matera was perhaps the most important.

This first stage took place thanks to the advice offered by Alberto Cottica, founder of the Modena City Ramblers and an expert in an innovative form of local development that was based on total openness to proposals from below. These were gathered in a broader perspective of

---

[1] Greg Clark, *Cosa succede in città. Olimpiadi, Expo e grandi eventi: occasioni per lo sviluppo urbano* (Milan: Il Sole 24 Ore, 2010).

"community," with the daily actions of individuals connected by a technological backbone of open data, usable by all and continuously renewable. The mapping of the community, the commitment of individuals to a new collectivity, the idea that writing software and using social media could increase the transparency of relationships and overturn a top-down policy model, instead giving ample space to a new bottom-up model constituted a new utopia. In this open and accountable society, the leading politicians in each region would not not have to tell people what to do, but would rather build implementation platforms that would allow community proposals to be tested, acted upon, and implemented.

The first round

Starting with the European, primarily Anglo-Saxon, concept of community, we gradually delved back into the history of the city and the Mediterranean. In Adriano Olivetti's concept of "community," artists and writers were at the service of society and the economy, working together to generate a new form of wealth that was based on the sharing of skills and energies—not just the accumulation and redistribution of money, but rather an ever-new but lasting agreement focused on doing things with others.

Since the 1950s, such a model had seemed to be projecting itself very appropriately into the Euro-Mediterranean. At a time when the economic crisis of 2008 and the increasingly evident climate crisis were calling everyone to their responsibilities as individual citizens and consumers, attentive not only to their own interests but also to the broader ones of a humanity on the verge of collapse, those of us planning the candidacy of a small southern city as European Capital of Culture felt these issues were central. Evidently such a utopian approach was perceived as valid by the thirteen jurors who read the first twenty-one dossiers that arrived in Rome in September 2013. It was thanks to Matera's contribution, entitled *Insieme—Together*, that the city was included on the event's shortlist, along with five others: Cagliari, Lecce, Perugia, Ravenna, and Siena. All of them were trying to bring something new to the Italian cultural debate, privileging planning over the enhancement of existing heritage—a choice that caused the exclusion of important and interesting centers such as Venice, Urbino, and Mantua, to name a few, which had shown not what they wanted to become but what they already were.

The finals

The six finalist cities were united not only by the decision to focus on a project based on the intangible and the intellectual status change that culture can bring to the daily lives of ordinary citizens, but also by an explicit pact: the creation of a collaborative network called Italia 2019, in which whoever won would have the role of "locomotive" and the others of "active and conscious wagons." This pact brought about concrete yet idealistic actions: The content creation process was shared, as was communication, and a total budget that was neither too much above nor too much below per capita measures was imposed. This latter measure served to force Matera's Ministry of Culture and Tourism to commit to a percentage of the final budget for the chosen city.

The year between the selection of the shortlist and the day of the nomination as capital city was so rich in initiatives that it deserved to take up almost half of the more than 400 pages of the book *The Invincible Cities*, by Serafino Paternoster, head of Matera's press office and of the candidacy.[2] The few pages here can only be a very condensed summary of that monumental work, which is composed mainly of all the documents that help us to understand the numerous and necessary administrative steps required to make a city a Capital of Culture. Matera distinguished itself in that year (November 2013–October 2014) not only through the extraordinary involvement of hundreds of citizens both in activities in the city and online, but also the establishment of a celebrated web team that kept the city's name and initiatives in the news. As an example, I want to recall the collaboration with the Superintendence of Artistic and Cultural Heritage directed by Marta Ragozzino, one of the great intellectual and operational engines of the whole Matera 2019 adventure. Author of much of the first dossier, Ragozzino was above all willing to test all innovations capable of producing new forms of community. These included the production with Virgilio Sieni and more than a hundred citizens of choreographic paintings inspired by Pier Paolo Pasolini's *The Gospel According to St. Matthew*, and the "Museum outside the museum," with the works of Carlo Levi being directly displayed in the homes of the city's most peripheral and popular neighborhoods.

2 Serafino Paternoster, *Le città invincibili. L'esempio di Matera2019* (Potenza: Editrice Universosud, 2017).

Matera anyway

Alongside the local team, the final dossier entitled *Open Future* was created by Joseph Grima, cosmopolitan architect, former director of Domus and of the Museum of Italian Design at the Milan Triennale, and inventor on behalf of the candidacy committee of the Open Design School, a school/non-school capable of dialoguing with citizens to produce original scenarios at the service of the region. Grima, together with Ilaria d'Auria and Alessandro Bollo, continued to listen to the needs of Lucanian creatives, reinforced the European dimension introduced by Rossella Tarantino, and introduced a series of stylistic devices that would be appreciated by the judging committee. Meanwhile, the local team expanded to the entire region, with Mayor Salvatore Adduce acting with Massimiliano Burgi to coopt all the municipalities of Basilicata to support the candidacy.

The foundation of the Foundation

It was again Scarlett Tarantino who had a decisive insight: It was not enough for the committee to win; it was necessary to transform it into a community foundation, capable of carrying on along the same path even if defeated. This operational move put the other candidates into check: Ravenna wanted to copy Matera but failed to do so, Lecce and Cagliari did not even try, while Siena was convinced of triumphing because of the intellectual brilliance of its proposal, written by Pier Luigi Sacco. With Salvatore Adduce, Scarlett drafted a framework resolution that made it clear that the nascent Foundation would have a budget of 25 million euro (exactly half the budget envisioned in the candidacy dossier). The dossier was broken down into nineteen measures, each of which linked back to a precise and compelling regional and European policy. If in terms of ideology Matera positioned itself as a new community city and in terms of artistic direction as a center of cocreation between artists and citizens, the challenge that immediately appeared was that of creative bureaucracy, an expression coined by a great supporter of Matera 2019, Charles Landry. It was also the first challenge it won.

What we talk about when we talk about governance

Creative bureaucracy is only possible if you have a very cohesive governance, capable of defining long-term goals and lining up a series of emblematic actions that convince citizens and the media that those goals are serious and achievable. Thus, alongside the writing of the dossier and together with the promotional work carried out in collaboration with many regional groups (alongside the APT Basilicata directed with genius and courage by Giampiero Perri, also worth mentioning are Sviluppo Basilicata directed by Raffaele Ricciuti, and the exceptional results achieved by the Lucana Film Commission chaired by Paride Leporace), Matera 2019 was characterized by close collaboration with productive enterprises and local media. Thanks to the talent of an entrepreneur such as Saverio Calia, longtime president of the Wood and Furniture Section of Confindustria Basilicata, the Matera 2019 sofa, in the shape of the candidacy logo, was made and taken to the most unlikely places, including to near the headquarters of Expo 2015, in the central Via Dante in Milan. Thanks to close collaboration with the local TRM network, a TV channel named TRM ART was born, reporting twenty-four hours a day on what Matera was doing to become Capital of Culture. Thus, acting on each of the four pillars of the candidacy (visionary dossier, citizen participation, creative bureaucracy, and bottom-up collective communication), Matera quickly approached the day of judgment, which was to be staged in Rome, preceded—as mentioned—by a visit to Matera by the judging panel. It was time for "The Seven Hours," not a film but rather a script that called for everyone to play a role, with the ostensible goal of impressing those who visited, and also aimed at making the citizens aware that theirs was not a dream but a great opportunity that could be realized. As October 7 dawned, everyone feared rain, which had already plagued the experts' visit to Lecce, where they had retreated to theaters instead of using the city's baroque spaces. In Matera, however, the morning air was crystal clear and on the Murgia, at the Belvedere in front of the oldest city in Europe, stood Mayor Adduce and Governor Pittella waiting for the European guests. After a brief greeting, they were left alone in the wind and the scent of thyme, and shortly after in the convincing voice of Pietro Laureano, who had already convinced the UNESCO world to make Matera the first World Heritage site south of Rome. The seven hours were recounted in detail on social media, with two moments in particular remaining in the collective memory. First was the meeting with all the mayors of Basilicata dressed in tricolor sashes at the entrance of Palazzo Lanfranchi, where Marta Ragozzino curated the incredible Pasolini exhibition already mentioned; second was the march of young people from all over the region to the city, led by the tree man, the *Rumita*, emblem of a timeless civilization. On the sidelines, everyone went to lunch with Matera families who had set the tables for the distinguished guests.

At the end of the visit, Matera was informally proclaimed capital of hospitality;[3] ten days later, on October 17 at 5 p.m., Commission President Steve Green and Minister Dario Franceschini officially named it European Capital of Culture.

In the trenches

The rest is history; but often good fortune means that projects become mythical and failures are forgotten. One remembers what works and accidents along the way are not considered ... but some points must be noted here, because the Matera affair did not stop on the day of the proclamation but began then.

With a title in its pocket, a budget that was almost completely agreed and available, and an organizational team that had proved itself, Matera was on the starting blocks, ready to go. But history is not linear; it proceeds in leaps and bounds, and pitfalls lurk in the pages of unread books, in unspoken words, and in meetings that do not take place. So it happened that the mayor who won the title thanks to his administrative knowledge and his passion for ordinary people was not reelected by a few votes; a member of the organizing committee defeated everything the mayor had approved, ran for mayor himself, and won at the ripe old age of eighty; and then the new mayor asked for the resignation of the "foreign" director and failed to get it. The wind that had propelled a city under full sail into the future seemed to turn it upside down: Buoyancy was lost, the mast holding the sail broke, rain swept the deck, and everyone felt like retreating to drink hot punch while they waited for the storm to pass...

---

3 In 2022, the international audience of Booking.com declared Matera the most welcoming city in the world.

Passage to the Southeast (Brussels uber Alles)

In 2015, the Expo in Milan was ending as a resounding and unexpected success, and in Matera the initial enthusiasm seemed to have died down. The mood was that of the sadness that follows a hangover. Great works were announced, but the idea that people are more important than bricks was lost. It was the people themselves who wanted infrastructure in the first place, and you can't blame them. The ruling class, which until a moment before had seemed to back a revolutionary project, seemed to need a good reason to put Matera back on the map: It was uninterested in content, and only praised building projects. All the collaboration melted away like snow in the sun. Perhaps the project was too difficult, the language too European and remote from local dreams and needs. Perhaps the vanguards need to be defeated in order to generate new ideas. It appeared to be enough to settle for victory. But Brussels wanted to know what was happening: Did that provocative and idealistic Matera that had put the citizen at the center of cultural life still exist?

Agreements are to be kept

Fortunately, the dossier that Matera had submitted to the European Commission in 2014 could not be changed. It was because of this dossier that Matera won, not because of its unparalleled beauty and originality, both natural and artistic. If that program had not been realized, the other five finalists could have appealed. This was what the Brussels envoys explained to the newly elected mayor Raffaello de Ruggieri, who had to accept the winning cultural project. Unfortunately, in this internal debate, the population's emotions grew colder, with the promises of both sides becoming grounds for confrontation instead of dialogue. Even the communication front, which has always been united, seemed to stress the crisis—dealing a blow to the credibility of the program, undermining the ability to bring on board national sponsors, and risking the cancellation of preagreements with important Italian and foreign artists. It was 2016 and the hands were ticking inexorably. Would the South, with its human warmth and its desire to return to the center of public life with a sophisticated and elegant project, risk see its fate compromised by an excess of envy and individualism?

The second coming (feat. John Niven)

Attempting to unravel the tangle was the rector of the University of Basilicata, Aurelia Sole, who with great skill kept the municipality and the region, the political and the organizational sides, at the table. Institutional architectures were dedicated, statutes were dismantled and reassembled, regulations were rewritten. This did not look good, but the myth of the "opacity" of the Matera 2019 Foundation was born. If nothing was shown, it was because very little was produced. Fortunately, the desire was maintained that the project would be carried out by protagonists of the local creative scene, the so-called project leaders who were entrusted in cocreation with the Foundation team with about 50 percent of the cultural program. They were sent around Europe, meeting potential partners, participating in intensive training courses, and collectively discussing both the proper administration of resources and innovative cultural indications. Those who had claimed that Matera 2019 was a "foreign" project were contradicted by the facts: Everything that became concrete activity had an appropriately local root and a strictly European matrix.

For two years, the focus was on the project leaders. There was a sense that the wind was going to change; that the storm that had hit Matera would pass. Finally, the new mayor had to admit that the Foundation was the only thing that was working towards completing the projects on time, as the national projects managed by Invitalia had been delayed (it would be interesting to explain why, but this is not the place). The incumbent majority was finally replaced by those who had managed the candidacy, with the former mayor who had given all the propulsive thrust to the candidacy being called in to govern the last phase of the event preparation. Thus, Salvatore Adduce, a longtime administrator, like a Churchill who lost an election then won the war, was appointed as the new president of the Foundation in the late spring of 2017. His old employees rejoiced, knowing that his irony, human touch, decision-making abilities, and great practicality would be the basis of the renewed confidence needed to make Matera the best Capital of Culture possible.

Those who work don't make love

A small facetious interlude. As Jonathan Coe writes in his amusing novel *Expo 583*, those involved in major events participate in a game that lasts an average of seven years and gives birth to but also leaves behind loves, friendships, passions, predilections. The pace is so relentless that it can be compared in the first phase to preparing for a marathon, then to high jumping, inefficiently, then to an obstacle course, where every day one runs a lap while always keeping to the thirteen steps. You can't keep up with the pace of institutions, of government administration, of rules. There is no planning that holds: Either you have too many people controlling everything, so the fixed personnel costs are too high, or you have a structure that runs like hares in March meadows, trying not to get caught by hunters. There is a solution: to outsource every activity, to have no structure, to employ only mercenaries; but then no real legacy is left on the ground. Because the real legacy is not the infrastructure, but the skills of the people—who often, to do their jobs well, for a few years forget family, friends, books, music, sport, and keep themselves tied to their desks, as Vittorio Alfieri did to finish writing his tragedies.

Materadio, or rather the medium is the message

Benefiting from Salvatore Adduce's return was the team that he, together with Rossella Tarantino, had forged and that had never stopped believing in the Matera 2019 project: in particular Marta Ragozzino, director of the Polo Museale della Basilicata, and the director of the Foundation (that would be me, Paolo Verri). We represented, the four of us, the gang of four some would immediately say, four different pillars: policy, territorial strategy, the national cultural institution, the widespread event, respectively. These four basic ingredients needed a voice, a smile, a megaphone that reached the right audience. For Matera 2019 all this was represented by Radio Tre, its director Marino Sinibaldi, and its outstanding staff. The alchemy between Matera and Radio Tre produced Materadio, which from September 2011 brought the best of national and international culture to Matera every year, through a festival that was born from the continuous dialogue between the two structures, improving the performances of both.

Thanks to Matera, Radio Tre became even more popular, widened its audience and its role, has been able to promote projects that are less niche but even more innovative. Thanks to Radio Tre, Matera 2019 has been able to define its audience from the very beginning (participatory listeners, willing to turn into protagonists and to not be passive, have become the city's true temporary inhabitants).

Materadio in 2018 completed the relaunch of the Foundation, which had begun on January 19 of that same year, with the presentation of half of the cultural program made official exactly one year before the inauguration of the event. This was a necessary race against time to prove to everyone that there was no delay, that the political blockade had not damaged either the quality or the potential impact of the project. The theme of Materadio 2018 was unsurprisingly local/global—as if to say: Here in Matera, we can build a mediation, we are not afraid of over tourism, we want to play the long game, once again all together, citizens, creative class, organizers, twin cities, sponsors, media. The big concert by Max Gazzè that opened the manifestation at the Tramontano Castle got everyone into the right mood: The promise was that every day would be the same, full of stimulation, joy, cheerfulness, and also the ability to deepen and share. The morning before the opening of Materadio, Mayor de Ruggieri, Foundation President Adduce, and Director Verri, all three interviewed on stage by Marino Sinibaldi, handed over to the minister for cultural heritage and activities the official program for Matera 2019, a volume of over 300 pages that matched each project hypothesis described during the candidacy five years previously with concrete actions that were distributed throughout eleven months of activity, from January 19 to December 20. Even the budget was secured. For the first time in Matera's history, major sponsors such as TIM, Intesa Sanpaolo, and Enel put up money to make the former shame of Italy the stage for Europe's most important cultural event.

Stabilization

Open the future

The day of the inauguration soon arrived: January 19, 2019. The launch event was attended by Italian president Sergio Mattarella, Prime Minister Giuseppe Conte, European Commissioner for Education, Culture, Youth and Sport Tibor Navracsics, along with hundreds of other national and international guests. The inauguration aimed to sum up

2019's events; it extended over 200 square kilometers and was produced together with RAI, involving twenty foreign cities and as many towns in Basilicata, each of which hosted a musical band from a municipality that had already been or would be a European Capital of Culture. A production with more than 2000 musicians, actors, dancers (those who counted them swear it was precisely 2019!), which began at ten in the morning and ended past two the next morning, involved dozens of parades in all the city's neighborhoods, as well as community lunches in which people from far-flung backgrounds spoke to each other in gestures and managed to understand each other. From the best-known stars of the evening, such as Skin and Stefano Bollani, to musicians in a band from a tiny village in Lucania, everyone hugged, everyone lit lights and extinguished fears, everyone cried with joy and endured the downpour that for an hour tried to ruin everything, making the live broadcast of the grand circus finale in Vittorio Veneto Square less beautiful but no less touching.

Since that day, with a multiplier effect that had been perceived as early as October 17, 2014, but which in 2019 became unstoppable, Matera has been talked about everywhere. Many desired effects have been accomplished, but there have also been many unlooked-for ones. Matera is an example of the urban paradox: the fact that the strengths generated by redemption and revival are at the same time weaknesses. We have seen, for example, that making citizens proud of the place where they live brought about revenge against the ruling class that had planned and led the candidacy, as if citizens could control their own destiny without any representation. It is difficult to operate the project and provide the tools to understand it at the same time. It was planned that more meetings would be held, giving even those who had not personally participated in the process a way to feel part of the team. But it is utopian and even unfair to believe that everyone will agree with innovative designs that sometimes use complex mechanisms.

Media, partners, gurus, and others

What is unquestionable is that the message Matera 2019 wanted to send certainly resonated with the media world. The idea that the poorest city in Italy and Europe had become European Capital of Culture only sixty years after a forced exodus had taken more than 20,000 citizens away from their traditional homes, had a GDP growing by 1.5 percent per year, that house values had appreciated by more than 50 percent, that real estate transactions matched those in Korea, that in five years there was been a fivefold increase from 100,000 to 500,000 visitors and that the number of beds for visitors increased from 2000 to 10,000 in ten years—all these are incontrovertible facts. And they are reflected in the international visibility measured by the Foundation in its first five months of activity in more than 21,000 press clippings, more than 1.6 billion people contacted, 180,000 attendees at the more than 450 events organized, 300,000 attendees in the city, plus 60 percent attendance in the region and 30 percent attendance in Matera, but also 15 percent in the province of Bari. These numbers were almost triple what were promised on July 19, 2017, when the call for at least ten sponsors was launched—numbers that make one wonder how much more successful the event could have been if governance had been effective and if the planning of collective actions for promotion and reception had not stalled on the field of mutual envy.

Among the most effective partners, the efforts made by RAI to better communicate Matera 2019 should be noted. It is difficult to plan a year of programming, but public broadcasting succeeded not by creating a fixed Expo-style structure, but by following Matera with almost all its tools: with information first of all (from Tg1, which paid constant attention to the cultural program and provided very detailed reports, to Tg3 with a weekly segment that has the highest listening share among similar programs), but also with the production of an original monthly magazine program, *TeleMatera*, brilliantly hosted by Edoardo Camurri, and with a constant radio presence, not only Radio Tre but also Radio Due. At the European level, the agreement with Euronews, the most important news network in Europe, which used its platforms intelligently and produced a series of highly visible and high-quality specials, paid off. Excellent impetus was given by Ferrovie dello Stato, the state railway, which was an extraordinary media partner both in terms of screens offered and articles in the periodical *Le Frecce*, and high-end sponsors, among whom Intesa Sanpaolo stands out: A campaign that constantly promoted Matera 2019 used the displays of its more than 20,000 ATMs throughout Italy.

Matera has become ubiquitous in national and international communication. An observer of the world of media and innovation, Luca De Biase, has said: "Matera has been able to fascinate and involve everyone, to be both sympathetic and influential. The highbrow cultural proposal has no conflict with the desire for a clean and simple city that makes itself loved as a place in which one may above all walk in open-air spaces."

The year that came

When the long-awaited challenge year arrived, it became clear, even to those with event experience, that eleven consecutive months of activity—if taken seriously—are indeed extreme. The Universal Expositions, which run for a maximum of six months, are difficult to maintain throughout at the same pitch and with the same validity. For Matera 2019, seven different types of audiences had been imagined so they could be offered distinct yet competing content over the months to define the overall mood of the event. Ordinary citizens, school children, journalists and information mediators, experts, and workers in the world of culture, promoters of the tourism sector, the business world and visitors: Each of these spheres required distinct projects, meetings, and involvement. And at the Foundation, there were only 70 people, not 700, more than half of them very young, who had arrived through a selection process called "Makers & Linkers," imagined precisely to enable the construction of innovative cultural contents and the opportunity to speak to distinct factions of the public.

This thorough work was potentially a source of enormous conflict with the many administrative rules, which were themselves often conflicting. Some individuals could do some things and not others, and it was not at all easy to select them through calls for proposals, or even by asking them to sign up to a portal. And if all this produced enormous delays in event construction, it must be recognized that it generated equally enormous openings: People who might never have imagined undertaking particular cultural work are passionate enough to jump in, learn about the problem, and then solve it.

It was clearly demonstrated that Matera 2019 was initially a laboratory: a laboratory of content, with more than 80 percent of the activities built from scratch on the ground through the involvement of Italian and European workers (the latter exceeding 50 percent). It was a communication laboratory, as we have mentioned already; a social laboratory, which saw more than 15 percent of the population (an impressive percentage) directly involved in the construction of events before they came to fruition.

The inaugural ceremony as well as the project *Chiamata pubblica for Dante Alighieri's Purgatorio* carried out by Ravenna Teatro, as well as Mascagni's *Cavalleria Rusticana* staged by Teatro San Carlo under the direction of Giorgio Barberio Corsetti, built piece by piece with the citizens of Matera, were leading examples of a new cultural system that had been put in place. That system has succeeded in attracting tourists (drawn primarily by the notoriety that the winning bid bestowed on Matera, they are often satisfied just by walking through the city), but above all it has revolutionized the role of the public—who in Matera 2019 were involved before and during, rather than just afterwards. It was a concrete example of a community making a project, not enduring it.

Future

Legacy

What is left in Matera after 2019? If we were not too demanding of ourselves, too submissive to the economic dimension of existence, and knew how to really enjoy life, the urge would be to shout, "Nothing else is needed!" These wonderful years changed the very idea of the city. Many things have worked, many have not. That's life; that's beauty, one could write. But a sense of responsibility dictates instead that we should at least quickly review the new strengths and weaknesses that Matera has acquired in the ten years since the European Capital of Culture project began.

Matera today is well known. It is a prime destination. There is much quality tourist accommodation, which has been provided without building new properties but basically by restoring large existing houses. There is a truly enviable interior design style owing to the expertise of the former furniture-making district. It has some new cultural spaces and others that will be opened in future. It has a new university campus that is currently much larger than necessary, but has the space to grow into a real hub of knowledge and innovation. There is a new road that connects the city with an airport that has grown in services and destinations in just forty minutes. It has a substantial national and international network. There are people capable of organizing great events. Of course, it has much more; but these are the elements that are already very important and distinctive.

Five years after the closing ceremony of the event that changed its history, Matera continues to surprise. On the one hand, thousands of visitors who discover it recommend it to friends and family; on the other, a solid social dispute persists over the city's future, quality of life, housing costs, and entrepreneurial capacity. On the evening of December 19, 2019, when the warm and unforgettable words of David Sassoli—President of the European Parliament, who passed away far too soon in January 2022—resonated in the ears and eyes of those gathered at the Cava del Sole, Matera felt itself at the heart of Europe. And it was. The pandemic, between 2020 and 2021, not only interrupted the tourism growth trend but also forced reflection on whether everything that had been built in the city was above all for visitors, and not also—and above all—for residents. The cultural citizenship passport, invented by the organizers of Matera European Capital of Culture, signified precisely this: that a city earns the title of capital of culture because it produces culture (not buys it, not imports it—and if it does, it asks those who come from outside to engage consciously and durably with local citizens), and especially if citizens, in addition to co-creating cultural content, become its regular users in a logic of permanent role exchange.

This tendency—central to the candidacy process and fundamental to the year's success, recognized by external observers as one of the most faithful to the original project—was not, however, maintained as a defining element in the city's subsequent path. Although a group of citizens independently drafted a manifesto for participation and cultural co-creation—drawing above all on two major projects: one on Dante's *Purgatorio* with Ravenna Teatro, led by Marco [name missing] and Ermanna Montanari, and another on *Cavalleria rusticana*, driven by director [name missing]—and another group quickly set up a volunteer cultural association entirely independent of the institutional organization, political debate detached itself from what had taken place, reverting to a strong sense of restoration by concentrating decisions and activities in the hands of a few. Those excluded from the candidacy process sought revenge rather than convergence with the newly launched models, weakening them. The wealth generated by the title and the success as a tourist destination drove up prices and expectations, while the sense of community from which it all had begun fragmented—reproducing, in a town of just over 60,000 inhabitants, what had happened in Turin after the Olympics in a city of over a million.

As after the victory of the title in October 2014, the political community, instead of making a pact to renew what had been developed during 2017–2019, tried to individually exploit the results, bending them to partisan rhetoric. Some even claimed, forcefully, that it was a relief the "hangover of 2019" was over and that now life could return to normal—as though it were possible to deny or forget what had happened.

What certainly did happen was that governance of the Foundation, once the capital year ended, passed into the hands of the Basilicata Region; and that the government in office failed—as Sassoli himself had repeatedly suggested and urged—to make Matera not only a media symbol but also a concrete example of new forms of urban development, especially for the South.

This double perception—of outsiders enchanted by the city's beauty and innovative projects, and of residents who can hardly wait for everything to return to normal, to a life shaped by tranquil rhythms, extreme simplicity, and essential but excellent services—is, in the end, the true dialectic of contemporary cities, which have yet to find a perfect synthesis between these two aspirations.

Matera, by recently choosing as mayor Antonio Nicoletti—already the designer of many city initiatives under Raffaello De Ruggieri's mandate and a respected director of APT Basilicata—now seems to want to forge such a synthesis: one in which quality of life, cultural authenticity, and the attraction of talent, businesses, and tourists are not in conflict but can and must converge powerfully.

9 Tokyo
Old people and children

A city halved—and crisis

When *Speed Tribes*, Karl Taro Greenfeld's book about Tokyo's urban tribes, came out in 1994, the West seemed to awaken from the mythology that the Japanese people had managed to build after the horrors of World War Two: that they were a pacifist people, obsessively devoted to work and family; a people exceedingly respectful of rules and manners, almost to the point of being boring. It seemed impossible that in parallel with these recognized identities, in the neighborhoods farthest from the Imperial Palace, or on rainy nights by the waterfront and in the hotels that housed thousands of multinational company managers by day, an exaggerated deviance was expressed, through biker gangs dressed like American Hell's Angels, kilos of traditional and synthetic drugs, and gigolos and young Lolitas on offer.

Yet by the late 1980s and the beginning of the last decade of the century, something sensational happened, well observed by the careful and rigorous scholar Saskia Sassen among others. The global economy had exploited the enormous growth of the metropoles to create an unholy pact between finance and urban transformation, aimed at making the new areas that were under construction especially in the great Asian metropolises the future counterweights for the planet's major banks and insurance companies. Twenty of these major institutions, that is, more than 50 percent, were not coincidentally based in Tokyo at that moment in history.

Wealth seemed to flow freely, and as before the 1929 crisis in the United States, the underworld began to take its place in the urban geography and imagination of the younger generation. After three centuries in which such imagery had been dominated by the figure of the Shogun and in which conservatism, including architectural, had been the hallmark of Japanese urban culture, from 1960 onward the image of the Japanese person—somewhat like that of the West German a generation after the end of the war—became that of an extraordinarily mild person with well-defined schedules and a desire to save. The near-total destruction of Tokyo between 1943 and 1945 had allowed for complete urban restructuring; only Berlin and Dresden underwent greater damage than that caused by ten months of repeated air strikes on Tokyo. In particular, the bombing of March 10, 1945 caused a feeling of total desolation, made even more tragic by what happened in Hiroshima and Nagasaki on August 6 and 9 of the same year. The capital, which had seen uninterrupted growth since 1868, with the population doubling between 1920 and 1940, was physically split in two, and the number of its inhabitants fell from just over 7 million to just under 3.5 million.

Relaunch

However, the effects of the war did not prevent Tokyo from returning to over 7 million inhabitants in the 1950s and stabilizing at between 11 and 12 million residents between 1975 and 2000.

The continuous reconstruction of urban spaces, coupled with an exceptional development of transportation infrastructure, such as the high-speed railway (Shinkansen) inaugurated a few days before the 1964 Olympics, created a veritable urban continuum that is comparable in some ways only to Los Angeles, a city with which Tokyo is mirrored on the other side of the Pacific Ocean.

The engine of Japan's formidable revival (apparent in Tokyo along with five other major urban areas) is that the capital city has a governor rather than a mayor, and its GDP is as much as that of a medium-sized European state, such as Belgium or Sweden. It is striking, and deserves some attention, that three out of five of the city's most recent governors have had a very high-profile literary education, as if in Tokyo narrative has an established precedence over reality. This serves to reinforce the image of an autonomous city that is capable of great challenges but also of great moments of collective depression: a true world city that is not a place inhabited by citizens from dozens of different nationalities (as is the case for London and New York), but a place of extraordinary interest because its ethnic composition is so compact and so seemingly homogenized.

From the 1960s to the late 1980s, with the speculative bubble of 1991 acting as a watershed between then and now, it is more the lifestyles that have changed than the shape of the city, which has gradually expanded with continuous cellular reproduction but without ever forgetting traditions, indeed using them as points of reference and eventually adding new ones. The crisis of the very early 1990s brought with it a series of questions, but also new opportunities not only and not so much for a city that feeds abundantly on itself, but also for citizens who have seen their ideals change from that of the employee of large private enterprise, the salaryman also willing to karoshi for the company, that is, to die from overwork, to an existence much more centered on individual needs, seeking a new balance between interiority, work, nature, and culture.

Tokyo is thus open to a new definition of citizenship that is of interest not just to observers of Japanese culture but to those who in widespread urban phenomena see signs anticipating social trends that will spread all over the planet. The confidence in the city that took the form of a desire to buy even small but easy-to-reach housing, well connected by the almost endless subway and bus lines, gradually turned into fear with the crisis of the 1990s, even though there was no serious unemployment (rather it was wages that lost value, with an average decrease of 5 percent between 1995 and 2005). The leading economy with a widespread sense of superiority is experiencing the challenge of Korea, with large brands such as Toyota and Sony competing with new giants Samsung and Hyundai. What is most impressive are the social statistics: One in four fifty-year-old men is unmarried (it was one in a hundred in 1964!), but only two in a hundred children are born out of wedlock (in Italy this figure is twenty in a hundred, in the Netherlands forty).

A new idea of the city, capable of holding together the metropolitan system and a city-state dimension with the habits, traditions, and passions of the inhabitants of Tokyo, as well as creating new opportunities for them, was badly needed. Unlike with cases such as Pittsburgh or Turin, it is not easy to reconstruct all the relationships that led to a new urban community project that was based on diversity rather than homogenization and the enhancement of certain social extremes, especially demographics. Attention to children, the elderly, those with disabilities, and more generally the effort to give a different role to women have been at the heart of the revitalization of Tokyo, which today, thirty years after that epochal crisis, feels completely reinvigorated but also matured both as an urban space and in terms of the society that inhabits it.

Compared with other large Asian urban areas, Tokyo has a very well-established history as a metropolis. As Giorgio Piccinato recounted in his *A World of Cities*,[1] the 1920 census (the first of its type in Japan) attests to a population of around 4 million for Tokyo; "fifteen years later, it will be 6.4 million, about the same as London and New York." Tokyo thus poses itself as the representative of the Asian continent in the confrontation on the one hand with North America, in which New York plays the leading role, and on the other hand with old Europe, holed up in Old Britain, with the continental capital of London that, in spite of its decision never to enter the European market definitively, holding on to the pound, right-hand drive vehicles, and pub opening hours, gradually senses that it can become a world capital if it opens up to the hundreds of ethnic groups that inhabit it—more than New York itself can accommodate.

In short, Tokyo has always been a hub of world development, more so than Beijing and Seoul, which in recent years have also expressed extraordinary capacities to produce content and above all wealth. Tokyo is style, reference culture, and its crises are our crises, crises of growth, crises of relationships. Tokyo is one of the cornerstones of a planet that, even in the 1960s, was very large, one in which it was difficult to imagine knowing—and even more so visiting—every continent and every state. (This same planet has for some months, by contrast, seemed too small and taken for granted, so much so that a requirement for new discoveries and new challenges has grown in us.) Tokyo has created its own mythology of a super-technological city, home not only to the most important manufacturers of machines for technical reproducibility (its karma is that of transistors, white-coated employees creating huge "brains" capable of helping human beings amid strings of 0s and 1s), but also of spaces in which these innovations become an integral part of everyday life. The Team Lab Borderless, set up in Odaiba, the old port of Tokyo, is a large

---

[1] Giorgio Piccinato, *Un mondo di città* (Turin: Edizioni di Comunità, 2002).

new entertainment space created by the engineers/artists of Team Lab, and is one of the most interesting cultural production collectives in the world. It perfectly reflects the trend that we will come back to at the end of the chapter: Old people and children, the protagonists of every visit, will also become the protagonists of a new, more mature idea of the city.

Stabilization

Of the approximately 1,700 cities in the world with a population of more than 300,000, as many as 56 percent are at risk of being exposed to a major natural disaster. Of the six types of natural disasters identified by the United Nations, Tokyo is at risk from three, so it is only natural to think of the city's revitalization as beginning with its ability to withstand and, indeed anticipate, potential crises arising from a clash between natural elements and urban management. In the 2016–2020 planning document, which came into effect in 2017 and was signed by then-new governor Yuriko Koike (the first woman to assume this role in the city's and the nation's history), the issue of security was at the forefront–not unlike, and perhaps emblematically, Istanbul's strategic plan.

Tokyo chose three penguins to identify the city's three lines of development; this is partly because these birds are very social, and also because in each of their vast and highly organized colonies there is always one that dives into the water first to show the others the way. Tokyo's three penguins point to the three types of city that citizens are invited to build together, following those who are willing to lead the way: a safe city, a city in which everyone can lead a busy and profitable life intellectually as well as economically, a city that is dynamic and fashionable.

Safety is not a crime-related issue: Japan is the country with the seventh lowest homicide rate in the world, and family- and work-related lifestyles lead more to problems of depression and isolation than to clashes between citizens or collective forms of deviance. Being safe really means countering earthquakes, fires, and floods. After the disaster caused by the 1923 earthquake and the destruction wrought by World War Two, the Japanese imagination was severely tested by the March 11, 2011 tsunami. This was measured as the fourth most violent earthquake in the history of the planet, the most terrible seismic tremor in the history of the island of Honshu, which was shifted several meters toward the United

States and waves up to 40 meters in height. The damage amounted to $210 billion, there were more than 15,000 confirmed deaths, and there was the declaration of a nuclear emergency, the first since 1945, with very serious effects for the two Fukuyama power plants.

This is why between 2014 and 2020 work has been done to further increase the capacity of houses to resist earthquakes (the mean is expected to increase from 83.8 percent resistance to 95 percent!) as well as fires (with an increase from 61 to 70 percent), including through the promotion of new housing. At the same time, efforts have been made to increase the number of volunteers among the special fire brigades, which have decreased because of the aging of the population. Special attention has also been paid to the increase in torrential rain, the effect of which in recent decades has been seen not only along Atlantic coasts but also in areas usually less stressed by bad weather, such as European cities. The actions envisioned are a greater ability to collect water in a much shorter time than a decade ago, and to quickly and effectively map and share via smartphone the areas that are at risk of even partial flooding. Finally (and the blood runs cold when comparing this with the bridge collapse that happened in Genoa in 2018 and those that have taken place more recently in many other parts of Italy), Tokyo plans to redevelop more than 160 bridges and 26 underground tunnels in just three years, as one in three is more than fifty years old.

Insisting on tireless and continuous redevelopment of the city is not unusual for either Japan or its capital city. Tokyo has always adopted very stringent housing reconstruction measures: The average lifespan of a private building in Japan is about twenty-seven years, about one-third the average age of a private building in Europe. Indeed, extraordinary maintenance is required every thirty years, making it preferable to tear down and rebuild rather than renovate buildings. This standard, which was initiated so that buildings kept up with earthquake resistance and fire-fighting technologies, has had profound effects on the continued growth of the construction industry, as well as on the proliferation of architectural and design skills, with a continuous mixing of styles in the different metropolitan neighborhoods.

Indeed, in crossing Tokyo, one gets the impression that much that matters is expressed in the actions, in the forms of each person, which are understood as ways of communicating one's respect for others, one's feeling to be part of the state, first and foremost. It is natural, then, that the issue of resilience with respect to the challenges between urban areas and natural disasters is at the center of policies and actions that are taken to improve the competitiveness of the capital and the nation.

Alongside the issue of infrastructure comes that of a new role for more mature citizens—not old people, as the average life span fluctuates between seventy-nine for men and eighty-six for women, but rather what we might call "seniors." By 2022, 56 percent of them are still expected to be employed, and the city itself is working to find suitable jobs for the more than 16,000 in this group who are seeking them each year. Roles are emerging that are based on their ability to care for and nurture children, with only an apparent role reversal: The silver economy is secured by the presence of young families who have economic growth potential that is associated with both parents being able to work full time, and thus the need to find adequate accommodations for their children not just during school hours.

Future

Tokyo, with a series of very specific actions, aims to become the world's number one city in the Global Power City Index, the ranking compiled by the Mori Foundation and its Institute for Urban Strategies,[2] aiming to rise in ten years from seventh to first position, which for now is firmly in the hands of London.

In the 2021 edition of the ranking, Tokyo is for the sixth consecutive year third in absolute value (after London and New York, followed by Paris, bypassed in 2016, and Singapore), fourth for economic development, scientific research, and capacity for cultural interactions, fifth for accessibility, only ninth for livability (but up from previous years), and

[2] The Global Power City Index (GPCI) "evaluates and ranks the major cities of the world according to their "magnetism," or their comprehensive power to attract people, capital, and enterprises from around the world. It does so through measuring 6 functions—Economy, Research and Development, Cultural Interaction, Livability, Environment, and Accessibility—providing a multidimensional ranking. The GPCI is able to grasp the strengths, weaknesses, and challenges of global cities in a continuously changing world not only through a ranking, but also through analyzing that ranking's specific components" (https://mori-m-foundation.or.jp/english/ius2/gpci2/index.shtml).

still far from the podium (seventeenth) for environment. Despite a great deal of effort not only by the government but also, and especially, by the private system towards this end, Tokyo ranks only eighth in its ability to attract top-level managers (it is fourth for skilled workers). Finally, it should be noted that the city has improved its "Trendsetting Potential" owing to hosting the Olympics in 2021.

If one cross-references this data with some still very weak social elements—such as, for example, the very low number of women at the top of public and private companies, with Japan in last place for this on the Global Power City Index—it becomes clearer what the purpose of the Olympics was. This position was strongly desired by everyone and was defended by Abe Shinzo until the day before he resigned as prime minister because of stress from overwork, becoming a metaphor for the world that Tokyo has dominated, with a very strict and all too damaging effect on both people and the nature around them.

Tokyo envisions itself in 2030 as being a much more open city, the active center of a network of twelve world metropolises with which it has historical relations: indeed, New York, Beijing, Paris, Sydney, Seoul, Jakarta, São Paulo, Cairo, Moscow, Berlin, Rome, and London have had twinning agreements with it since 1960 (the agreement with the British capital is the most recent and dates from 2015). However, this network and the activism of numerous actors involved in international relations are still not enough for the city to be perceived as a place that has the urban potential to allow international talent to reside there easily and mutually beneficially. Even the university system is still perceived as too nationalistic, and Japanese universities have for many years given way to Chinese universities as entry points to markets for innovation, production, and exchange of expertise.

While in smaller cities (as in the case of Wrocław, which isn't even as big as a district of Tokyo) one can implement specific operations that stand as acting on the entire urban system, in the case of megacities the implementation of urban policies is not direct but has to involve morally persuading stakeholders. Emblematic of Japanese culture is the fact that citizens are addressed directly, and even a new typical day can be envisioned for them, replacing the one to which millions of Tokyoites (the preferred term is *edokko*, children of Edo, the city's ancient name) have been accustomed for more than half a century. This new day includes a sharp increase in smart working (well before its global spread as a means of reducing contagion during the pandemic), more attention to personal time, more responsibility given to men for household affairs, and more active living for women, who are credited with significantly growing local productivity and thus the economy as a whole.

To reach first place in a challenge that is being played out against three other historic world cities, New York, London, and Paris, Tokyo chose, as mentioned, a classic method: hosting a big event, or rather hosting "the" big event, the Summer Olympics. Scheduled for 2020, this was postponed for a year owing to the pandemic, similarly to the Dubai Expo and many other international events. Like the 2008 Beijing Olympics, the 2021 Tokyo Olympics served first and foremost to remind the world of the efficiency and kindness of the Japanese, and to show everyone ten new areas that had been created in the largest metropolitan area in existence (pending the exponential growth of one of Tokyo's twinned urban centers, Indonesia's Jakarta, which is sooner or later expected to surpass it in population, but is already well ahead of Tokyo in the percentage of young people).

From north to south, Tokyo has decided that some of its districts should specialize in attracting new talent and new tourists, in its aim to become the most visited city in the world, and to enhance its trendsetting in fashion, design, and culture. Just to give a few examples, which are by no means exhaustive, the Ikebukuro district, located in the northwest, is dedicated to art and culture, acting as a geographical counterweight to the already busy cultural center of Shibuya. Otemachi and Yaesu, north of the port and in the area formerly occupied by Haneda Airport, is destined to host international companies and new creative industries, with a totally rethought urban look and feel. This visionary project redefines the Tokyo we know in terms of a new balance—between the Baby Boomers who are now over sixty and the gaming generation, who are living in two parallel worlds, often without realizing the differences between them.

The acronym to identify this whole process, which on the one hand estimates to increase the annual number of tourists to the Japanese capital from 15 million to 25 million in ten years, and on the other has the goal of increasing from 54 to 70 percent citizens' satisfaction with their life in the city, could only be FIRST: Finance, Innovation, Rise, Success, Technology. Until just a few weeks before their inauguration, the Olympic Games could have represented the final downfall of an imaginary that made Japan the equivalent in the East of what Italy represents in Europe:

an overly bureaucratized state, with excessive public spending and an antiquated cultural model when compared with Korea's, as well as difficult economic management and an inability to strengthen its presence in world markets, as China has done. But the Japanese, with the self-sacrifice that makes them an unsurpassed model of loyalty both to state and community, believed to the last in the Olympic Games on which they had so much riding. The design detail established as elements of success strategies that are usually not closely related to the worlds of sports and entertainment, such as those designed to promote the role of women in society; while new models of infrastructure, necessary to revive Tokyo as the heart of the entire country, implemented unprecedented models of tourism that were closer to the needs of visitors, without provoking roars of disapproval from the citizenry—as had happened not only in Barcelona, but also in Amsterdam and Copenhagen. Innovation, in turn, was ensured by the simultaneous creation of special economic zones in which international companies could collaborate with local businesses through dedicated development funds. A special advisory board was even tasked with promoting original models of finance applied to local growth.

The main innovations envisioned for the 2021 Olympics were linked to the entire country's desire to excel once again through technology. Smartphones came to the rescue of all those who might somehow encounter language barriers during their stay, with applications such as voiceTra, developed by the National Institute for Information & Communication Technology, translating conversations and allowing people to request street information and make purchases or restaurant orders in as many as twenty-seven languages. The massive use of 5G offered better connectivity, with all the benefits in terms of direct digital access. Another challenge met was the presence of robots in the Olympic village as assistants for competitions and sportsmen, just as a driverless driving system was implemented in the cab sector. The event was also an opportunity to go green, with fleets of electric buses and new hydrogen-powered trains. Fifteen years after the Expo in Aichi, the island near Nagoya that was first the capital of the kingdom of Japan and the general headquarters of Toyota (not coincidentally twinned with Turin), Japan managed with the Tokyo Olympics to anticipate the challenges of the urban future with a mix of technology and kindness.

All this was made possible, again paradoxically, by the absence of the public, particularly the international public: All these services were tested almost exclusively by the so-called Olympic family, that is, all the participants in the competitions, together with sports officials, journalists, and the world of economic investors. The numbers were not small, but were certainly not those that had expected when the city applied for the event in 2011; nevertheless, the games were watched by more than 3 billion people, and in a summer that saw much of the world's tourism practically at a standstill, with a temporary revival of very strong, manned national barriers, the Games constituted the planet's main spectacle. The organization was called flawless by all, but what stood out most was that these Olympics–so technological, so prepared to use innovative tools–also turned out to be humane, and the relationships between the athletes would have thrilled De Coubertin. Suffice it to recall the decision of Simone Biles, considered the greatest gymnast of all time, not to participate in the finals because of an inner feeling of discomfort that meant she would not perform at her best, or the sharing of Olympic gold by the two men's high jumpers, Qatar's Mutaz Barshim and Italy's Gianmarco Tamberi.

The style of the Japanese Olympics, which could have lacked warmth and emotion, with only the voice of the TV commentator to make up for the lack of roars from the benches (as was the case, for example, in some team sports games that were played without an audience), conveyed to us a fundamental element in Tokyo: confidence. Watching the Olympics, we realized the passion, the rigor, the sincerity of a nation's design proposal. We admired the many young people who collaborated as volunteers and their exchange of ideas and opinions with their elders; as well as the absence of strong contrasts in a city that is as large as an entire region and yet knows how to make a few essential choices understandable to all.

The new challenges toward 2050

Although the Olympics were held without spectators, the experiment was a great success—so much so that Governor Koike Yuriko, born in 1952 and thus emblematic in both age and outlook of the large generation of Japanese women born during the post–World War II baby boom, was re-elected in March 2024 for a third term. Together with her coalition, she was able to develop a new plan for Tokyo's future titled *Tokyo 2050 Strategy – Unlocking a Better Future*, which identifies 26 key goals to keep Japan's capital at the forefront of urban innovation in the 21st century.

Building on the core theme first introduced in 2011—when preparations were underway to host the 2020 Summer Olympics—namely the new roles that both the young and the elderly were expected to play by 2030 and the strong collaboration between these two groups of citizens, the city plan presented by Tokyo's Strategic Department in March 2025 takes us straight into the future of global cities. It addresses who will inhabit Tokyo—and indeed the entire planet—by 2050, and even includes ambitious suggestions for the 22nd century, offered without hesitation and with a certain pride, to the local community as well as to international investors and visitors from around the world.

What may be possible in 2125 thus becomes not merely one of many potential futures, but the foundation for shaping the time between now and then.

To prepare for these new and extraordinary challenges, the next ten years in Tokyo will see the community at work through three major approaches:

1. Strengthen partnerships with diverse actors to address challenges.
2. Collaborate with cities around the world to solve common urban issues.
3. Mobilize policies to establish a trajectory toward a sustainable future.

In particular, a major development strategy will be promoted based on the 3 Cs: Children – Chōju (Longevity) – Community, in collaboration with all the municipalities of the greater metropolitan area, which brings together over 21 million inhabitants. As the governor explained in a passionate address at the World Urban Forum, the goal is to develop pioneering, transdisciplinary initiatives in collaboration with universities and local organizations—integrating the knowledge produced within those same institutions to generate innovative projects useful for the future of Tokyo and other global cities.

In her greeting, the governor stated:

> The Grand Reform of Tokyo is unequivocally moving forward. However, our times are changing at a dizzying pace. Structural issues in society, including a declining birth rate and an aging, shrinking population, are growing more acute. This is no time to be letting up on the pursuit of reform.[3]

---

[3] See the Governor's greeting at: https://www.metro.tokyo.lg.jp/governor/goaisatsu

The Tokyo Metropolitan Government web page further emphasizes:

> We will tackle any and all challenges head-on and work to further accelerate measures under the *Grand Reform of Tokyo 3.0*, my updated vision for metropolitan administration reform, in order to make Tokyo into the best city in the world.[4]

This underscores the role of knowledge as the true engine of urban areas—but, more importantly, the awareness that only in cities can we create the antidotes to an increasingly common belief within national systems: that society is beyond reform, locked into wealth derived from competition between companies protected within "closed" markets. Tokyo instead positions itself at the forefront of a new vision of society, one where everyone consciously shares the benefits of university research in order to live not only longer, but also happier lives.

Fittingly, the first two of the 22 strategic actions toward 2035 aim respectively to ensure that over 85 percent of children under 18 smile every day, and—perhaps even more importantly—that over 70 percent of them believe, with confidence, that they can change society through their efforts and actions. A unique example on the planet, and one that, hopefully, will serve as a model at the global level.

---

[4] See the Tokyo Metropolitan Government website at: https://www.english.metro.tokyo.lg.jp/

Conclusions
Putting cities back in the hands of the citizens

> From the thirteenth century on, the dread of plague prompted a periodic exodus from the city; and in that sense, one may say that the modern suburb began as a sort of rural isolation ward. Even today, in a survey of the suburbanite's reasons for moving from Cleveland to the outskirts, the largest percentage of reason in favor on this move, 61 percent was "to live in a cleaner, healthier neighborhood. [...] In every age, then, the fear of the city's infections and the attractions of the open countryside provided both negative and positive stimulus.[1]

This beautiful quote from Lewis Mumford's *The City in History*, published in 1961, initially soothed me, but then made me feel even more like Achilles chasing the tortoise. If the paradox works for the relationship between mayors and their urban communities, between experts and cultural workers, then there is even more reason for it to affect the thoughts of those who—like yours truly—have been thinking for the past two decades how to make the citizens of a community happy. How do we create the conditions in which citizens can become communities? How do we abandon parochialism, make projects that bind without adding constraints, that give courage without hubris, that tend toward development without excluding, giving confidence to those who until recently were left behind?

The victories of cities are like the happiness in Eugenio Montale's famous poem, "Felicità raggiunta": They are like threads of the blade on

---

[1] Lewis Mumford, *The City in History: Its Origins, Its Transformations, and Its Prospects* (New York: Harcourt, Brace & World, 1961).

which with difficulty we walk; the nine stories we have read are not and cannot be definitive. A city—like any living organism—cannot say "I made it"; especially not now, after a global pandemic that, as Zygmunt Bauman reminds us, has produced both confidence and fear, but also necessitates a planet on the one hand increasingly controlled and on the other less capable of generating real social innovation.

Times are looming in which cities, contrary to what has been written recently, will be under even more pressure—especially those Italian and European cities that are able to offer quality hospitality while treating the virus in a way that leaves little space for fragile freedoms.

I have visited all the cities mentioned here several times, and everything I have written is the result of a personal relationship with these places. They are cities that I love very much not only for what they say, but also for how they plan, how they challenge the future. In addition to the three Italian cities that have each made up a third or so of my working life, the three European and three non-European cities were chosen after I was able to talk with, for example, the mayor of Istanbul atop the Topkapi Palace and the founders of Pittsburgh First.

The narrative must conclude. I would like to procrastinate, to weave the web again now it is early 2022, almost two years after virtually all the rest of the book was written. Having waited for the pandemic to wane, here is the classic mistake of Achilles surfacing—trying to catch up with the tortoise. The demigod, fast, almost unbeatable, has a human heel. Just shoot the arrow toward that one place, and Achilles is finished; the tortoise, ancient inhabitant of the planet, can move just a little, and once again, victorious, cannot be caught.

The myth of perfection, of a balanced society, of a responsible relationship between power and democracy, between wealth and redistribution, is in the midst of a crisis; and if there is a place where this myth at once is celebrated and fulfilled, yet self-destructs, that place is the city. From Giorgio Piccinato's 1970s journey to non-European metropolises, to Saskia Sassen's economic analysis in the 1980s; from Richard Rogers' community cities to Charles Landry's creative cities; from Edward Glaeser's urban triumph to Ben Wilson's eternal metropolises, urban literature has been gradually enriching itself, constructing new imaginaries that the next ten years will bend to the ever-approaching experiences of the metaverse and digital currencies. Perhaps private states and public states—for instance, the major players on the world economic and political scene—will have to find new balances. Part of this challenge will be played out in conventional space, including on the seas (where competition similar to that of the seventeenth and eighteenth centuries is regaining a foothold), but it will also happen online, whether in immensely large spaces, or in the confines of a video game that is experienced on a tiny screen, yet connects dozens of young lives to give life to temporary microcommunities.

Yet this will all still translate into urban space.

People will choose where to have a family, where to study, where to have fun based on the narrative of individual cities, their ability to construct positive perceptions, in which physical elements combine with the services offered and the networks that individual neighborhoods, streets and buildings and lights and voices, are able to offer. Each state will still have its capital; but if the state is not there, the city will not fail—quite the contrary.

This transformation will not be quick. Urban civilizations, utopias that become reality even in apparently impossible geographic realms (as Emanuele Felice showed when presenting the case of Dubai),[2] cannot be summed up in a newspaper article, a tweet, an insider's newsletter.

As this book has tried to show, cities on all continents are the engines for all forms of contemporaneity; and communities are more often than not unaware of this as they perpetually search for a favorable destiny without knowing how to anticipate it. They ask the different forms of government to interpret their instances, more often than not to a mayor who knows how to interpret them using in part their own direct experience, and in part drawing on a vast pool of examples to make use of thanks to collaboration with those who have experienced this before.

Thus Turin has attempted to transform its industrial experience in the light of Barcelona's experience; thus Istanbul has realized it can be a powerful hub that connects West and East as in the previous century was Cairo's role; thus Pittsburgh chose science and technology and learned from Boston how to generate added value from research to counteract the medical crises that arose from a twentieth century of fire and metal. Regardless of size, small and medium-sized cities, such as Matera and Wrocław, have imposed themselves on the recent European narrative by

---

[2] Emanuele Felice, *Dubai. L'ultima utopia* (Bologna: Il Mulino, 2020).

transforming their own shames into strengths for rebirth; destructions that become bridges, evacuations that are an appeal for new models of living.

Awareness of the public–private coalitions that drive these transformations may have different temporal measures and political coherence. It may arise out of opportunism (and may yield to the infamous beat of envy and power for its own sake) or out of more thoughtful awareness that no mayor, not even the most intelligent and valued, can lead alone; yet it cannot be short-term: Change has to have a long-term perspective.

Cities must necessarily rely on a double register—on a music that has a daily rhythm yet is nevertheless embedded in a symphony.

The work of the growing number of "urban practitioners," that is, experts from different disciplines who come together in teams to solve existing problems or, better yet, to anticipate problems to come, will never detach itself from urban realities, from what Tim Marshall calls "the power of geography." But this power derived from location now has new opportunities.

Francesco Erbani, intervening in the national debate on the role and future of the suburbs, has published a book entitled *Where the City Begins Again.*[3] It is in the suburbs that this occurs, Erbani explains, because they are the places in which it is easier to experiment, and where it is often more profitable to do so than in historical centers or established cultural areas. Having read the *Atlas of Cities*, edited by Paola Piscitelli,[4] we could extend this argument from Italy to the rest of the world, comparing cases such as Bucharest and Caracas, Johannesburg and Mumbai. Like a living body that can be analyzed in every vital component down to the smallest cellular element, large metropolises are divided into very small portions, and the central question that emerges is always the same: "Who decides? Why? Are you aware of the choices?"

In 2012, Iolanda Romano, Italy's foremost expert on participatory planning in urban areas, published *What to Do How to Do. Deciding Together to Really Practice Democracy.*[5] That book, together with an import-

---

[3] Francesco Erbani, *Dove ricomincia la città. L'Italia delle periferie—reportage dai luoghi in cui si costruisce un paese diverso* (San Cesario di Lecce: Manni, 2021).

[4] Paola Piscitelli (ed.), *Atlante delle città. Nove (ri)tratti urbani per un viaggio planetario* (Milan: Fondazione Giangiacomo Feltrinelli, 2020).

[5] Iolanda Romano, *Cosa fare come fare. Decidere insieme per praticare davvero la*

ant article by Pierluigi Sacco that appeared in 2013 in the *Journal of Behavioral and Experimental Economics*, dedicated to cultural participation as a determinant of individuals' behavior change, still seems to me to be a vital element to be addressed in these last (but not conclusive) pages.

Despite the fundamental role of mayors, their charisma, and their leadership, favorable medium- to long-term results cannot be achieved without a consensus that is built on strong citizen participation. Often it is major events that provide the occasion for this participation, which can and should be turned into pride in one's city. If events are successful, they do not incur any or many of the frequent obstacles that can characterize them: for example, overly large economic interests that yield unexpected returns, or envy and jealousy among political leaders. But often in urban areas, the most important issues do not have unambiguous solutions, and need a debate that cannot be confined to the halls of politics but to reach individual citizens. Representative democracy, with its bureaucracies, often puts a considerable moat between itself and those who vote, which appears in the eyes of most to be insurmountable. We are helped by deliberative democracy, the special opportunity that gives, as Habermas puts it, "legitimacy to public action." This legitimacy is increasingly necessary and, according to Iolanda Romano, helps to construct a consensus that is not forward-looking, that does not have the exact timing of digital news or politicized politics (they are two sides of the same coin) but has very precise rules. It is a matter, when possible but especially when making major choices, of not allowing decisions that will affect the long-term good of the community to be imposed from above; the community has to be involved in discussing the issue according to a set timetable and in defined places, suggesting options, and taking the final decision according to a vote that involves a representative portion of the citizenry.

Following three stages, the presentation of a project, debate on it, and the final decision on whether and how to implement it, deliberative democracy brings the choice process to the center. Recently, we have seen an option prevail that we conveniently call "populist," but which we perhaps should call authoritarian: It involves either quick scrutiny by the authorities or a cursory analysis by the media that makes people lean toward one rather than another decision. One could conveniently argue

---

democrazia (Milan: Chiarelettere, 2012).

that as long as we have electoral laws that provide for delegation, it is hard to see why we should not regularly apply the concept of accountability: I voted for you, you were elected, you make your choices according to your conscience on my behalf; if your decisions no longer please me, I stop voting for you. Yet especially in contemporary cities, while this is consistent and valid, it does not seem to me to what we see happening every day. We are still trying to figure out what kind of city we want; there are many choices, and most citizens are totally excluded from the decision-making paths—so they become more and more disenchanted with daily democratic life. Frequently, the promises made on the campaign trail that are brought to the finish line by a mayor are not just disregarded, but set aside as soon as the eventual runoff is concluded. Building stadiums, shopping malls, university sites, defining the route and schedules of transportation, investing in one economic sector rather than another: Why not make the process of deliberative democracy the mainstay of these choices? It is not difficult to step back and lay proper foundations for choice, a choice in which a select few citizens represent the interests of all and take charge.

This is a process that scholars such as Paolo Vineis and Luca Savarino, the former a professor of epidemiology at Imperial College London and the latter a professor of bioethics at the University of Eastern Piedmont, also consider. In a recent volume devoted to the pandemic (*The Health of the World: Society, Nature, Pandemics*),[6] they remind us that choices for our future need a holistic vision: One Health, One Ethics. "How is it possible to recompose the endless disputes coming from a wide spectrum of cultures?" they write;[7] not only through our political representatives, but also thanks to ordinary citizens called to discuss and hypothesize solutions through the possible and necessary sharing of information and insights.

These are actions that may seem symbolic—and they are. But their symbolism is necessary, potentially complementing another tool, that of strategic urban planning, which was prominent between the early 1990s and the end of the first decade of the 2000s and now languishes in need of renewal. Yet in Italy the resources linked to the National Resilience

---

[6] Paolo Vineis, Luca Savarino, *La salute del mondo. Ambiente, società, pandemie* (Milan: Feltrinelli, 2021).

[7] *Ibid.*, p. 188.

and Recovery Plan urgently require a framework of objectives that can be shared at the macrolevel and discussed publicly—as has happened, for example, in France on the issue of climate change (mentioned by Vineis and Savarino)—and then to be integrated with a strategic vision that involves the development of large metropolitan areas on the one hand and rural areas on the other. The haste to spend has allowed projects that are very often dated or of marginal value to be pursued just because they are ready, while new and real needs that have not been planned for will not become part of the next three-year public spending plan that seems to be crucial for the revitalization of the Italian system.

A planned and fully participated-in urban future, both in Italy and much of the rest of the world, appears to be a desire that contrasts with another, dominant, imaginary: Urban areas today seem to largely resemble the city in which the protagonist of *Ready Player One*, Steven Spielberg's film released in 2018 (based on the book of the same name by Ernest Cline, who also contributed to the film's screenplay), lives. The cities in which people live with great economic and relational difficulties are almost destroyed, but none of this is perceived by the citizens, who live almost perpetually in a parallel universe, that of video games. The first, extraordinary, opening scene that takes us to 2045, the year in which the film is set, sticks in the viewer's mind for a long time. In order to design new cities that function well and provide security for most of their inhabitants, even at the expense of the freedoms that they usually expect, will we have to take refuge in virtual reality? Will this be the next frontier of the urban paradox? Abandoning real space for the so-called metaverse? As mentioned earlier, this will only happen in a city. Will this be Korean? Chinese? African? European? Spielberg again takes us to his home, to an ordinary US metropolis. This time, Achilles is a boy who is skilled at solving gaming issues and the turtle is a community lost in the ultimate struggle between good and evil. The paradox continues...

Bibliography

Bagnasco, Arnaldo, Giuseppe Berta, and Angelo Pichierri, *Chi ha fermato Torino? Una metafora per l'Italia* (Turin: Einaudi, 2020).

Barbera, Filippo, Andrea Bocco, Antonio De Rossi, Marco Guerzoni, Patrizia Lombardi, Paolo Mellano, Alessandra Quarta, and Giovanni Semi, *Torino 2030. A prova di futuro* (Rome: Luca Sossella Editore, 2021).

Barca, Fabrizio, and Enrico Giovannini, *Quel mondo diverso. Da immaginare, per cui battersi, che si può realizzare* (Rome-Bari: Laterza, 2020).

Baricco, Alessandro, *Quel che stavamo cercando* (Milan: Feltrinelli, 2021).

Bauman, Zygmunt, *La società dell'incertezza* (Bologna: Il Mulino, 1999).

Bauman, Zygmunt, *Fiducia e paura nella città* (Milan: Bruno Mondadori, 2005).

Boeri, Stefano, *Urbania* (Roma-Bari: Laterza, 2021).

Brugmann, Jeb, *Welcome to the Urban Revolution. How Cities are changing the World* (London: Bloomsbury Press, 2010).

Caffo, Leonardo, *Essere giovani* (Milan: Ponte alle Grazie, 2021).

Choay, Françoise, *L'urbanisme, utopies et réalités* (Paris : Editions du Seuil, 1965).

Clark, Greg, *Cosa succede in città. Olimpiadi, Expo e grandi eventi: occasioni per lo sviluppo urbano* (Milan: Gruppo 24 Ore, 2010).

Erbani, Francesco, *Dove ricomincia la città. L'Italia delle periferie—reportage dai luoghi in cui si costruisce un paese diverso* (San Cesario di Lecce: Manni, 2021).

Felice, Emanuele, *Dubai, l'ultima utopia* (Bologna: Il Mulino, 2020).

Glaeser, Edward, *Triumph of the city: How Our Greatest Invention Makes Us Richer, Smarter, Greener, Healthier, and Happier* (London: Penguin Press, 2011).

Greenfeld, Karl Taro, *Baburu. I figli della grande bolla* (Turin: Instar Libri, 1995).

Harari, Yuval Noah, *21 Lessons for the 21st Century* (London: Jonathan Cape, 2018).

Herodotus, *Histories* (London: Penguin Classics, 2014).

Kihlgren Grandi, Lorenzo, *City Diplomacy* (London: Palgrave Macmillan, 2020).

Landry, Charles, *The Art of City-Making* (London and Sterling: Earthscan, 2006).

Landry, Charles, *The Creative City. A Toolkit for the Urban Innovators* (London: Earthscan, 2000).

Lupatelli, Giampiero, *Fragili e antifragili. Territori, economie e istituzioni al tempo del coronavirus* (Soveria Mannelli: Rubbettino, 2021).

Manzini, Ezio, *Livable Proximity: Ideas for the City that Cares* (Milan: Bocconi University Press, 2022).

Marshall, Tim, *The Power of Geography. Ten Maps that Reveal the Future of the World* (London: Elliott & Thompson Limited, 2021).

Mumford, Lewis, *The City in History: Its Origins, Its Transformations, and Its Prospects* (New York: Harcourt, Brace & World, 1961).

Pamuk, Orhan, *Istanbul. Memories and the City* (New York: Knopf, 2005).

Piccinato, Giorgio, *Un mondo di città* (Turin: Edizioni di Comunità, 2002).

Piscitelli, Paola (ed.), *Atlante delle città. Nove (ri)tratti urbani per un viaggio planetario* (Milan: Fondazione Giangiacomo Feltrinelli, 2020).

Quammen, David, *Spillover: Animal Infections and the Next Human Pandemic* (New York: W.W. Norton & Company, 2012).

Ratti, Carlo, *Smart City, Smart Citizen*, edited by Maria Grazia Matteri (Milan: Egea, 2013).

Rogers, Richard, and Anne Power, *Cities for a Small Country* (London: Faber & Faber, 2000).

Rolando, Stefano, *Public Branding. Per un nuovo modo di narrare i territori e le loro identità* (Milan: Egea, 2021).

Romano, Iolanda, *Cosa fare come fare. Decidere insieme per praticare davvero la democrazia* (Milan: Chiarelettere, 2012).

Rykwert, Joseph, *The Seduction of Place* (New York: Pantheon Books, 2000).

Sassen, Saskia, *The Global City: New York, London, Tokyo* (Princeton, NJ: Princeton University Press, 1991).

Schnapp, Jeffrey, *Digital_Humanities* (Cambridge: MIT Press, 2012).

Vineis, Paolo, and Luca Savarino, *La salute del mondo. Ambiente, società, pandemie* (Milan: Feltrinelli, 2021).

Vitellio, Ilaria, *Regimi urbani e grandi eventi. Napoli, una città sospesa* (Milan: Franco Angeli, 2009).

Wilson, Ben, *Metropolis: A History of the City, Humankind's Greatest Invention* (London: Jonathan Cape, 2020).

Zovi, Daniele, *Alberi sapienti antiche foreste. Come guardare, ascoltare e avere cura del bosco* (Turin: UTET, 2018).

www.ingramcontent.com/pod-product-compliance
Lightning Source LLC
LaVergne TN
LVHW050952080826
845145LV00005B/1488

* 9 7 8 8 8 3 1 3 2 2 8 3 6 *